Home Remedies, Cures and Kitchen Tricks

Home Remedies, Cures and Kitchen Tricks

by Ben Charles Harris

Gramercy Publishing Company
New York

Cautionary Note: The remedies, cures and suggestions contained
in this book are not necessarily medically sound or fail-safe
solutions. Therefore, they should be used with reasonable care
and diligence.

This 1985 edition is published by Gramercy Publishing Company,
distributed by Crown Publishers, Inc. by arrangement with
Crown Publishers, Inc.

Manufactured in the United States of America

Library of Congress Cataloging in Publication Data

Harris, Ben Charles.
    Home remedies, cures, and kitchen tricks.

    Reprint. Originally published: Kitchen tricks.
1st ed. Barre, Mass. : Barre Publishing, 1975.
    1. Home economics.   2. Cookery.   3. Medicine,
Popular.   I. Title.
TX145.H27 1985   640'.202   84-25314

ISBN: 0-517-463016

h g f e d c b a

Introduction

All the while I've been thinking and writing about culinary herbs and herbal medicines, I've had two themes: health and thrift. It seemed to me that these notions belonged—more than in any other place in the home—in the kitchen. Of course, we want to be healthy in the living room and thrifty when we're buying gasoline or mending our clothes. But the kitchen is the place from which our health (and our preventive medicine) comes. And since our food allotment is probably the largest slice of our budget, it's a very good area to be thrifty in. When you think about it, the kitchen is the most important room in the house, in terms of dollars and sense—health sense, that is.

So this book contains *kitchen tricks* for health and for thriftiness. I've written about ingredients probably found in your kitchen (and about some you might decide to include there) and about some preparations or processes that take place there (like saving food wastes for your garden compost).

I should say at the outset that this book is not the sum of my efforts alone. While many of the money- and timesaving ideas are from vivid recollections of my childhood days, I've obtained far more of my kitchen tricks in the past 35 years by asking various audiences to send them to me. These contributing experts are the real authors. Hundreds of ideas were sent by listeners to my radio programs. I received numerous other hints from members of farm groups, from church and garden clubs, from those who attended my lectures and herb-study classes, and from many readers of my books and magazine columns. Also, during my 32 years as a druggist, I was rewarded with suggestions by many of my customers.

Health should be enjoyed and maintained by doing things the right way in your kitchen every day. Don't wait until the doctor insists that you cut out salt and harsh spices and that you cut down on meat and sugar. Live healthfully every day and minimize damaging foods. (See X-RATED FOODS for my list.) Avoid processed food (often nonfood), minimize overly acid food, especially at night. To preserve nutrients, minimize the cutting and the cooking of foods. Eat small meals! Don't overtax your digestive system and avoid thereby the dangerous excess weight that strains the heart and indeed all organs. Rest. Try fasting on a regular basis (for directions, see FASTING). Try growing some of your own food (organically, of course). And use delightful, healthful herbs in cooking and in your teas as daily tonics and digestive aids. (Suggestions for herbs abound in this volume.)

This work features:

1. *Foods.* One must know when to buy them, *which* to buy, their preparation and preservation; how to use leftovers and how to incorporate them with other foods. To the health-minded, certain foods are permissible, others forbidden. Some cooking habits are not only corrected but improving health.

2. *The kitchener's many helpers and timesavers.* They appear as little tricks and big ideas that erase the boredom and oppressive atmosphere from the kitchen. Try to follow through on the many warning Thou-Shalt-Nots and on the health-protecting advice.

3. *Food seasoning hints.* Many are actually the much-practiced suggestions of high-salaried chefs. *No:* salt, white vinegar, or harsh

spices like mustard or pepper; *yes:* pleasant savory herbs (thyme, marjoram). Growing your own aromatics in the sunny backyard or in flowerpots offers a constant supply of *fresh* herbs for a salad dressing, bouquet garni, soups, casseroles, and so on. If your seasonings are store-bought, write to the packers for free, taste-tantalizing recipes. (Write also to packers of dried fruits and vegetables, cereals, molasses, and canned foods. Visit your local County Extension Service for available free informative literature).

4. *General hints for do-it-yourselfers.* You will save many more dollars by preparing countless items in your own kitchen laboratory. Homemade preparations are inexpensive, contain no allergy-producing ingredients, no dangerous or possibly harmful chemicals, and are as near to you as the pantry shelf. For instance, vegetable oils and avocado offer softening/soothing qualities to the skin and hair. Astringents appear as strawberries, cucumber, lemon, and witch hazel extract.

Example of a simple remedy: New or used tea bags to stop mouth or tooth bleeding and as an eye lotion.

Example of a household aid: An insect repellent composed of powdered cloves, red pepper, borax, and sulfur.

With the cost of living spiraling heavenward, one must learn to stretch one's income by not neglecting the small mounds that soon become mountains. For instance, you can cut your water bill in several ways. Keep a bottle of water in the refrigerator rather than waste a lot of water by letting it run until cold. A slowly dripping faucet can waste 15 gallons a day, a fast drip, 25, and a slow stream, 200 to 300.

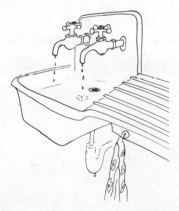

Shopping for food can exhaust your income if you buy product after product on impulse. My entry under SHOPPING details some things to be careful of. Whenever possible, buy at wholesale discounts from a local distributor. Unusually large purchases should warrant a price reduction: get this value by buying cooperatively with several other families. (See CO-OP)

Prepare your shopping list at home. Include none of the "luxury" foods such as ice cream, desserts, TV dinners, carbonated drinks, and candies. And don't be misled by food promotions and huge displays of *canned* fruits and vegetables or by the supermarket's 8,000 items. Do buy those weekly advertised "specials," but resist the nonessentials. Points to remember: Buy foods when "in season" and in good supply. Buy only as much fresh produce as you and your family can use in the next 2 or 3 days and store easily. *Read the label* of every product. Beware those foods with ingredients marked *synthetic, artificial, preservatives, coloring,* and *sweetening* agents.

Take your lunch to work. Plan your meals so that everyone eats at one time. Eat the produce of your own vegetable garden. Learn to bake bread, or buy "organic" bread in a health food store (more food for your money) or from a local bakery. (Choose coarse whole wheat, rye, corn, or pumpernickel loaves.) Buying milk at the store is cheaper than having it delivered.

Also, make fewer visits to overpriced restaurants. Eliminating the coffee-and ——— break at work will save you $130 a year. Do try a fruit break. Eat a minimum of man-made foodstuffs: the processed, boxed, and "convenience" items, the snack/junk nothings, liquors (wine is an acceptable compromise), colas, and fruit drinks.

Another way of reducing food costs is by supplementing your store-bought foods with *free* salad greens, potherbs, root vegetables, fruits, and berries. In almost everyone's neighborhood, there abounds a limitless supply of easily recognized dandelion, milkweed, sour grasses, and wild carrot. And blueberries and blackberries wait to be picked and enjoyed every summer. (Your library has many books on edible herbs. See, for example, my *Eat the Weeds,* Barre Publishers, Barre, Mass.)

And those leftovers! Do they keep piling up and filling your refrigerator space? They should never be discarded as worthless.

Using leftovers teaches us to avoid their appearance in the first place by not preparing or serving too much of any food at one time. This encourages us to eat less and so save our health; good for dieters, too.

As for the kitchen, because it is the room from which health emanates, it should ever be a challenging, pleasant, and enjoyable place in which to work, rather than a source of irritation, drudgery, or constant boredom. The kitchen is naturally the focus of many activities. So make the most out of your kitchen. Observe some of the points herein presented and enjoy a challenging change of pace.

Let "a place for everything and everything in its place" become your motto. Old hat, but a tried and true energy saver. Write out your plan of action. First, start eliminating all or most of the needless junk, the bargain aluminum pots and pans. Store the accumulated junk only long enough for the next church bazaar or garage sale.

Let your pots and pans serve as decorative accessories. Suspend them over your range or counter or on those "wide open spaces." Use ornamental hooks or a wrought-iron pot rack devised especially for this purpose. Store the lids and covers on hidden shelves. Paste or tape a colorful decal or picture on the open spaces—walls, cupboard doors, refrigerator.

You'd be surprised how quickly a few bright-colored flowers will enhance a table setting.

Locate one or more hanging flower pots near the window area. Use the sills for several small pots of those everlastingly blooming flowers.

Many a kitchen serves as a communication center and a place to exchange family messages or "don't forgets." Members of the family inevitably pass through for one reason or another. Why not place a chalkboard hung in a picture frame near the phone? (Notes on paper tend to get lost.) The message, once noted and done with, is erased. Tinted, 8½ × 11 paper attached to thin cardboard and taped on the refrigerator will serve not only to receive messages, it will remind you of buying needs and certain impending chores. Children, too, may thus be reminded of a task.

Separate your errands, shopping visits, and social activities, and limit yourself to only three such activities a day. If, and when possible, try to car-pool shopping and PTA drives with neighbors or friends. Write yourself a note, listing the next day's doings, and place the note on the bulletin board.

In self-defense, it's never too early to teach young children intelligent spending habits. This also weans them from TV commercials, while teaching them a sense of family responsibility (and, in time, a better knowledge of food values). A good start: let youngsters buy two or three fruits or vegetables on supermarket field trips. And they should be encouraged to help set the table, serve the food, and clear, wash, and dry the dishes. At the same time, teach your children safety in the kitchen—pot handles turned to the side or back of the range, burners turned off when not in use, undivided attention given when heating fat or oil, no pan left unattended without a timer set to remind you.

The entire process should begin right in the classroom. Teacher could balance such vapid phrases as "See Spot run" with reading ads and labels, differentiating between canned and fresh foods. As Virginia H. Knauer, special assistant to the President for consumer affairs has stated: "Let's save our children from 'consumer illiteracy.' Let's immunize them against misrepresentation, trick packaging, fake markdowns, free gimmicks, 'bait' offers, and fear selling. Let's ask our local school boards to join in the campaign for our children's sake—and keep asking them until they do. . . . Let's teach our children to be smarter shoppers than we are."

Don't let danger lurk in your cupboard, especially if there are small children around. Either remove from the catchall storage area under the sink all poisonous and even semidangerous items such as ammonia, soap powder and pads, cleaning, bleaching, and sanitizing containers, and aerosols, disinfectants, and furniture polishes, or leave them there and key-lock the cupboard. Do this also with paints, pesticides, rubbing alcohol, and weed and insect killers (possible child killers, all). Accidental poisonings alone kill about 500 toddlers a year.

Since little folks can't read, parents must keep under lock and key all prescription drugs and patent medicines. The number-one killer of children is candy-coated children's aspirin.

The following hundreds of kitchen tricks and the many how-to shortcuts will help to enrich a householder's own health and economy. The skills will be acquired only in the actual doing.

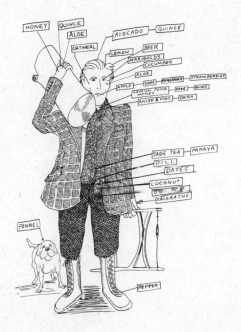

Thus, this work offers time- and money-saving ideas and budget stretchers, which should teach us how to live with less and within our means, how to think and act creatively and independently, and how to enjoy our everyday living in good health with the greatest return and personal satisfaction.

Every time you use a tip mentioned in this book, put a big nickel in the piggy bank and see how quickly you've saved enough to buy more books that will help you save your health, your time, and your money.

NOTE

You'll see symbols in the margin next to entries in *Kitchen Tricks*. These symbols are keyed to different broad categories of usage, so that if you're seeking information on, for example, medicinal uses of elements found on your kitchen shelf, you can find appropriate items by looking for an M in the margins. These are the symbols I have used:

F food
G garden
M medicinal
H household tips
C cosmetic
E etc., or miscellaneous

a

ALOE

Aloe is a nice house plant, easy to care for. If you keep a plant on • **M**
your sill, you have on hand a remedy for chapped hands, insect
bites, sunburn, scalds. Press the gummy juice from the leaves for
this medicine. For bad burns, a jellylike substance will hold better
to the skin. Prepare this with a solution of tea and Irish moss, then
add the gummy juice of the aloe.

ALUMINUM FOIL

If you need a trivet for a hot pot, wrap some foil around several • **H**
thicknesses of newspaper. Not unattractive!

Shaped foil makes a good emergency funnel. • **H**

Be very careful when you use aluminum foil near your electric • **H**
stove. Although it appears in sheets, this metal product is a good
conductor, which can give you the shock of your life if it makes
contact with any exposed electrical element of your kitchen stove.

ANISE

If you keep anise seeds and thyme on your spice shelf, you will • **M**
always have a cough remedy handy. Steep ½ teaspoon each of
anise seeds and thyme in a cup of hot water. Stir the mixture and
strain it when it cools. Add a teaspoon of honey to sweeten and to
help soothe the throat. Sip it slowly, a little every ½ hour or so.
This remedy is mild enough for infants.

Anise is also an old remedy for colic in babies. Mix ¼ teaspoon • **M**
each of anise, fennel, ground mint, and catnip in a cup of hot
water, or anise, fennel, and dill. Let it steep, covered, for 10

1

minutes. Stir it and strain, then re-strain through absorbent cotton. The baby may take it in a bottle or, if he will not, try a teaspoon. You might as well try it—you've tried everything else already, I'm sure.

ANTS

H • An ant problem may be solved by sprinkling about a mixture of powdered cloves and red pepper, with or without sulfur. Or prepare an old-fashioned but still effective insect or ant powder: mix thoroughly equal parts of borax, pyrethrum, and pepper. Dry the affected area and the threshold and spread lightly.

APPLE

F • An apple instead of a tranquilizer? A study at Michigan State University indicates that this works. The study, revealing fewer tensions, headaches, and emotional upsets, involved 2 apples a day.

F • Did you know that an apple a day can keep the dentist away? Apples play an important role in cleansing the teeth of decay-causing refined carbohydrates. The food removes debris, stimulates gum tissue, and also stimulates salivary flow.

F • Store apples away from onions and potatoes to prevent the absorption of their odors.

M • Apples can be a remedy for diarrhea: scrape the apples for babies, or simmer the parings in skim milk.

E • If your apples age before you can eat them, try drying them thoroughly and then carving them into faces. They can be attached to sticks and dressed. Apple dolls were a favorite toy in colonial America.

APRICOT

F • Be sure to remove the preservative sulfurous acid by soaking the fruits in cold water for ½ hour and then rinsing once again in cold water before eating. This is one of the favorite unsulfured foods of the long-lived Hunzas. Try eating the meat of the kernel.

ARROWROOT

That special arrowroot powder you bought for baby's weaning • **M**
formula or for the convalescent is easily dissolved in warm water
or milk. On cooling, it forms a jellylike tapioca substitute. Arrowroot is easily digested and is a gentle nutritive demulcent used
to help one recover from fevers and bowel complaints.

ASPARAGUS

Asparagus, like string beans, should snap when broken; otherwise • **F**
their freshness is suspect. If yours is the canned variety, open the
can from the bottom and carefully pull the stalks out by the
coarse ends. This prevents the tender tips from breaking.

Did you know that a juice extracted from the lower stems and • **M**
roots of asparagus makes an effective kidney remedy? Simmer 2
heaping tablespoonsful of the cut parts in 1 quart of hot water for
about 30 to 45 minutes—strain. Take a cupful every 3 to 4 hours.

AVOCADO

To hasten an avocado's ripening, put it into a brown paper bag, • **F**
or wrap a newspaper around it. Leave it thus for several days until
the skin color is no longer green.

If you use only part of this food, leave the seed imbedded in it to • **F**
prevent discoloration, or brush the open surface with lemon juice,
or spread a little butter or margarine over the cut edges.

The avocado is a highly nutritious, alkaline food offering 11 • **C**
vitamins and 17 minerals; but its buttery richness, owing to a 25
percent oil content, is thus obtained: Mash the golden-green pulp
to a creamy consistency and thin out with a little water, if necessary. Spread the cream over your face and, immediately after a
shampoo, massage well into the hair and scalp. Rub the inside of
the peel over other dry areas. Wait ½ to 1 hour before showering
or washing away the pap.

3

BANANA

E • Out of shoe polish? Rub your leather shoes with the inside of a fresh banana peel and wipe with a woolen cloth.

BASIL

F • A taste trick for tomato juice: powdered basil stirred into the liquid and chilled for an hour before serving.

BATH SCENTS

C • Something new and refreshing for your warm bath: Stuff a muslin bag full of the more pungent herbs, plus pine leaves, assorted mints, lemon balm, lavender, lemon and tangerine peels, thyme, rosemary, sassafras, and others of your choice. Place the bag directly under the slowly running hot water for a few minutes or until enough water has been admitted; then let the herb bag "season" the water until cool enough to get into the bath.

BAY LEAF

M • Use a minimum of bay leaves in your cooking. Large amounts of the leaves, berries, and oil are toxic. The leaves and fruits have rarely been employed internally except as a stimulant in veterinary practice. Middle Eastern peoples have used the berries as an abortifacient. The strong oil has been used as a pain reliever for sprains and bruises.

All members of the laurel family contain a powerful poison called • **E**
laurotetanine which acts like strychnine on the spinal cord. (Also take extreme caution against using the leaves of elder, wild cherry, and cherry-laurel, because of an added poisonous substance, hydrocyanic acid.)

BEANS

Soak dried beans in water overnight so that they will absorb • **F**
water and regain their predehydrated form. They will cook in less time, and the nutrients will not be lost.

To save money, buy navy and lima beans in bulk, usually in • **F**
Italian, Syrian, or Armenian stores.

Try serving beans cold and marinated as an extra vegetable dish. • **F**
Fancy, high-priced restaurants do. (Same with string beans and peas.)

BEER

Beer gone flat? Use it as a setting solution for the hair. First • **C**
shampoo and towel-dry the hair. Then dip a comb into the container of beer, apply directly to the hair, and lastly, roll the hair. Leaves no odor, so I've been informed.

BEETS

If cooked beets are not to your liking, try grating them raw • **F**
directly into a salad, or steam them and serve with parsley butter and a touch of lemon juice.

Beets help to purify the kidneys and liver, and their iron content • **M**
increases and strengthens the red corpuscles.

BEET GREENS

Beet greens are as important a food as the root itself, and, in fact, • **F**
contain many times the amount of vitamin A and of phosphorus as the beet. Yet a friend of ours, in a supermarket, watched the

vegetable counterman throwing the greens into the garbage. When my friend asked why, she was told, "Only poor slobs eat that!" Well, that middle-class counterman was denying his family good taste and good nutrition. I guess he was also denying his whole neighborhood (except for my friend, who insisted on buying beets with greens).

F • Like most other greens, beet greens should be steamed.

BIRDS

F • When my son Saul's pet canary, Tweety, entered our household, I recalled that Grandfather fed his chickens (as did the neighboring farmers) the seeds of weeds, especially stinging nettles. I found that most of the herb seeds were as good for the feathered creatures as for humans, so late in the summer Saul and his brothers and I were able to gather, only a few minutes from our home, large quantities of the seeds of foxtail (wild millet), yellow dock, lamb's-quarters, wild buckwheat, plantain, and, yes, ragweed. All these seeds later provided an excellent protein-rich ingredient for soups, bread, and cookies. Thus we began another sideline— gathering and drying edible seeds for fanciers of homing pigeons and other birds. Lamb's-quarters have a twofold purpose: they provide good nutrients and have anthelmintic (worm-expelling) properties. Of my "secret" formulas, the one that would almost guarantee a bird's returning to its cote and owner, contained peppergrass and wild caraway. We had erected our homemade, squirrel-proof birdhouses, one on each side of the garage and the side porch, two at different levels on the huge maple tree, and one on the spruce. Friends had offered blue jays, sparrows, and other birds large chunks of suet and fatty beef trimmings, but our vegetarian fare would not permit our doing the same. Other friends grew several bayberry bushes in their rear lot after noting that during the winter months the myrtle warblers were quite fond of the greyish white fruits. Actually the "wax" of bayberry is a true vegetable fat and hence as nutrient-filled as it is digestible.

Any excess of mountain-ash fruits that remained after we made our jelly and sauce was sparingly distributed to the benefit of robins, bluebirds, and woodpeckers. And having been advised that robins, bluebirds, and cardinals enjoyed sumac berries, we were able to gather enough of those fruits for them and their cousins and their aunts.

We saved (almost) all the seeds of melons and squash, which we dried, and added the seeds of wild-growing sunflowers and flaxseeds from my pharmacy; these became another meal for the visiting flyers. And at times we shared our raw (ground) peanuts.

The kitchen is an excellent area around which to place feeders. Or • **H** build out platforms from the outside windowsills. Birds often become hungry at the same time as humans and we've breakfasted together—I, in, and the birds outside.

A mailbox on a smooth, thin pole makes a good catproof feeder.

BLUEBERRIES

To obtain the optimum food values, always eat the fruits fresh. • **F** When the berries are uncooked, the blood-fortifying minerals of calcium, phosphorus, and iron, as well as manganese, are easily and quickly assimilated. The same holds true for the vitamin content. When you prepare a pie or pastry with this fruit, you diminish its food value.

Did you know that the early American colonists used milk in • **E** which berries had been boiled to paint their houses? Grey, not purple.

BONES FROM POULTRY AND MEAT

The larger chicken or turkey bones and the smaller marrow-filled • **F** meat bones should be crushed and included in soups. They are strained out after cooking.

Grandfather would break them up again into smaller pieces and • **G** put them deep into the garden soil as an excellent fertilizer for the garden. Dry them thoroughly, break into small pieces, and incorporate with soil at the bottom of a compost pile.

BOUQUET GARNI

F • The mention of a *bouquet garni* in your cookbook refers to a bunch of fresh (or in a pinch, dried) herbs, tied together in cheesecloth, which is cooked with the food and removed before the dish is served. The herbs: parsley, thyme, marjoram, savory, and rosemary.

BREAD

F • Baking bread? By letting your bread dough rise in a plastic bag, you can punch it down hard and knead it vigorously, since the dough doesn't dry out.

F • Loaves will yield a fine texture if the dough is frozen a day or two before baking. Be sure to let them rise before baking.

F • When baking, use organically raised, stone-ground flour. (We use soya, millet, rye.) But only flour enough as can be used within 4 to 6 weeks and refrigerate in an airtight container. Leave uncovered at room temperature for 2 hours if recipe calls for yeast.

F • Bread crumbs may be powdered via a coffee grinder or blender and used as a seasoning base. Hard or dried rolls and bread, including heels, offer a good source, so why buy? Separate into two or three portions. To each add a good pinch of a different blend of herbs. My favorites include basil, marjoram, savory, and oregano. Store the crumbs in your freezer.

F • Need dry bread in a hurry? Place a few slices on your oven rack and warm. The bread will dry out very well and will be quite crisp.

H • A heated knife blade will cut through fresh bread more easily.

H • You can often clean wallpaper by rubbing it with soft bread. Try it!

BROOM

H • To make your new broom last longer and sweep cleaner, slip an old nylon stocking over the ends of the bristles.

As a boy, I helped Grandfather make clothes brushes from as-   • H
sorted weeds and grass fibers. Today very few brushmakers use
indigenous twigs or plant portions. Country folk in the British
Isles, however, do use the erect and tough branches of the *cytisus*
herb, and of *ruscus* or butcher's-broom. Broomcorn or grass
(sorghum) is still used here, especially in the southern and western
states. The top of the stalk is cut 18 inches from the top, deseeded,
and quickly air-dried. At least one New England company I know
of makes brushes from the fibers of the palm tree and the Mexican
cactus.

BROWN SUGAR

Brown sugar, by the way, is not raw sugar. It is white, processed   • F
sugar with the molasses put back in. Most health-food sellers will
not sell brown sugar because they feel that although there is some
nutrition in the molasses, the chemicals used in refining make the
product dangerous.

Ways of keeping brown sugar soft: Put a piece of fresh bread in   • H
the container and close it securely. The following day you will
find the sugar soft. Or you may empty the sugar into a glass jar or
clean coffee can with plastic lid, add several marshmallows, and
close tightly. A cut-up apple works, too, as does a slice of orange or
grapefruit, or a lemon peel. The dried peel is replaced with a fresh
one.

BUTTER

Use only unsalted butter. Salt is harmful.   • F

Use butter sparingly. It is a real source of harmful cholesterol and   • F
future trouble.

The differences between butter and margarine are significant: • F
"Butter is better" has long been a favorite saying of mine, if only
because it is a natural product, and has a natural color when
freshly churned from sweet cream. While butter is considered a
saturated fat, it does contain an appreciable amount of *un*saturated fat to make it preferable to margarine and especially to

9

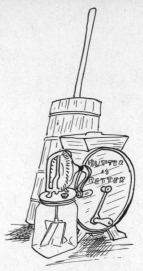

animal fats like suet and lard. It is a good fuel food, and since one's diet requires some fat, butter offers a source of such fat-soluble essential vitamins as A, D, and E. However, at high cooking temperatures, its unsaturated oils are lost and the other oils become oversaturated (and thus harmful). The rise in cholesterol is offset by eating a vegetable salad before or with the buttered food.

F • One tablespoonful of butter has 11 grams of total fat, of which 6 are saturated fatty acids, 4 are oleic unsaturated fatty acids, plus a minor amount of linoleic unsaturated fatty acids.

F • Further anticholesterol aid: Prepare your own butter blend by stirring thoroughly 2 parts softened butter with 1 part of safflower, sesame, or peanut oil and refrigerating the finished, blended product. For that purpose, I have also used herbed oils—vegetable oils in which aromatic seasoning herbs are immersed and warmed ever so lightly for a few hours and then strained.

F • Herbed butter: To a cup of melted, unsalted butter, add 1½ tablespoonsful minced or finely cut greens—garlic or onion tops, leeks, chives, parsley, chervil, or scallions. Season sparingly with the crushed seeds of dill or fennel, or ground leaf tops of dill, fennel, basil, or marjoram. Refrigerate several hours before using.

H • Butter will soften more quickly if placed on a dish that has previously been heated in the oven or has been rinsed in boiling water and dried. Or invert a warmed bowl over the butter.

10

BUTTERMILK

A facial treatment of gently warmed buttermilk counteracts • C
blemishes and oiliness. Apply warm in cheesecloth, allow to dry,
and repeat in 15 minutes. Rinse with tepid water, then with cold
water. This process cleans the area completely, is nondrying, yet
removes excessive oils.

C

CABBAGE

Small cabbages are usually tastier. • F

Trim the dark outer leaves of lettuce and cabbage as little as • F
possible and you save their vitamins A, B, and C, and minerals—iron, calcium, and potassium.

This food is best eaten uncooked with other salad ingredients. • F
The purple variety adds more color to a salad.

Serving cabbage as coleslaw is not recommended. Valuable nu- • F
trients are lost through cutting or shredding, and the moistened
mixture may have started to ferment long before it is consumed.
Accceptable if prepared 5 minutes before the meal.

The final touch to your own coleslaw if the seasoning with a • F
dressing base of herb vinegar plus celery seeds and ground marjoram or basil.

Avoid recipes whose preparation requires soaking a half or whole • F
head of cabbage in "salty ice water for an hour or so." Even cold
water leaches out the valuable minerals.

Before heating your roast at a higher temperature than usual • F
because you are in a hurry, wrap the meat in cabbage leaves and
fasten with toothpicks. An excellent way to retain the moisture
and heat. Eat the cabbage, too!

Freshly expressed cabbage juice has been used in the treatment of • M
peptic ulcers.

11

F • Early American sailors prevented scurvy by eating cabbage daily, though they knew nothing of its rich vitamin C content.

M • A modern writer suggests that a cabbage bruised leaf, dipped into warm water and applied to an inflamed or pus-discharging area, brings quick and amazing results.

M • Years ago a homemade cough syrup was prepared by boiling purple cabbage leaves in water and adding enough honey to thicken the cool, strained liquid.

C • Freshly expressed cabbage juice is much used as a cosmetic: it is cleansing, cooling, and slightly lubricating to the pores, especially for average to dry skin. Prepare a soothing lotion by simmering some cabbage with three or four slices of cucumber and a large handful of romaine lettuce in a stainless steel pot for ½ hour. To the strained liquid add just enough tincture of benzoin to produce a milky appearance. Apply after washing the face.

C • A cabbage leaf applied externally to the eyes will reduce inflammation.

C • To make a healing and soothing lotion, obtain cabbage juice by putting several soaked leaves through a juicer or by simmering them and a few pine needles in a covered glass or stainless steel pot for 20 minutes. Strain and add only enough Tincture Benzoin (obtainable at the drugstore)—1 or 2 drops at a time—to produce a milky appearance. Shake well before using.

H • **CANDLES**

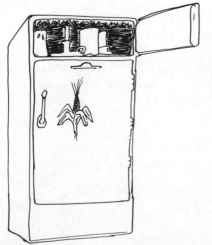

If you want to make candles burn more slowly and evenly with minimum of wax drippings, place them in the freezer for several hours—even overnight—before using.

Clean candles with a cloth dampened with alcohol. • **H**

CANNED FOODS

If the containers of canned foods are damaged in any way, do not • **F**
buy them. Reject those whose sides are dented (they can absorb
the chemicals in metals). Most important, however, is to reject
cans that swell on the top or bottom. The swelling indicates
contamination.

Get rid of the "canned" taste by simmering in canned liquid odds • **F**
and ends of vegetables and bits of cooked or uncooked poultry.
Or you may add ground cereals or cooked pasta—vermicelli,
spaghetti . . .

When your oven is on, you can heat an open can of vegetables by • **F**
setting it on the floor of the oven, thus saving time and no pot to
clean. Be sure to remove the label from the can.

Save the syrup of canned fruits in a plastic container and keep it • **F**
in the freezer until you have enough. Thicken it with a little
cornstarch and use it as a hot sauce over snow pudding, pound
cake, French toast, or pancakes.

Arrange all your canned foods alphabetically for convenience. • **H**
(Do the same with your household cleaners, furniture polish,
chemicals, and so on.) Mark the older cans with a crayon or
marking pencil so that you'll use them first. The longer canned
foods remain on your shelf, the more nutrients they lose. The
recommended shelf stay is one year.

CARROT

Raw food lovers have long put carrots in their juicer for a meal of • **F**
carrot juice, and I applaud the juice's nutritive benefits. But stop
at one glass and have something else for lunch, because too much
carrot juice can lead to carotenemia, a yellowing of the skin from
the pigment carotin or carotene.

13

CARROT TOPS

F • During the summer months, always buy carrots with tops, preferably at a nearby farm stand, and save the greens. For stew or soup, they are cut into ½-inch lengths and eaten with the other ingredients.

F • They may also be used fresh with other seasonings in a salad dressing or cheese spread.

F • Dried, they may be sprinkled over a soup, stew, casserole, or baked item when ready to serve.

F • Powdered, the green tops may be mixed with other herb powders such as marjoram, basil, and kelp to yield a most satisfying salt substitute.

G • Try growing the root in the kitchen window. Hollow out the center of a large root, tie a thin wire around or through the top, and suspend it in the sun. Keep the hollow filled with water. In a few days, the lacy foliage will appear and present you with a delightful hanging basket.

CELERY

F • Try dehydrating celery leaves. Wash them well and dry thoroughly. Once cleaned, they are dried at low heat in your oven. When dried, they're ground up and put into a clean jar.

G • To keep celery all winter, set it (with roots) in a box filled with soil and store in cellar.

M • Need a drugless sedative for nerves? Try the expressed juice of celery leaves and stalks in ½-cup doses, 3 to 4 times a day; or a warm infusion of the seeds (½ teaspoon) plus catnip (1 teaspoon). Good for insomnia, too.

CEREAL (see also GRAINS)

F • Leftover cooked cereal may be used in making muffins. For each cupful used, reduce the amount of flour in the recipe by ¼ cup and the milk by ½ cup. Use the cereal as an extender for meat loaf, fishcakes, and green pepper halves.

Leftover cooked cereal may also be molded in various shapes and, when firm, cut into slices and panfried. Serve them warm (like French toast) with maple syrup or honey. • F

CHEESE

Acceptable cheeses are those made from raw milk, which contain no coloring or preservative: Imported Swiss, Muenster, Colby, Longhorn, and Cheddar. Swedish Farmer's, Fontina, and Jarlsberg cheeses are made in Sweden without chemicals in the milk. • F

What's in processed cheese? Many chemicals have artificially thickened, homogenized, flavored, preserved, and colored it. Methyl cellulose is often the thickener, sodium carboxymethyl cellulose the stabilizer. A highly toxic chemical is sometimes added to cottage cheese to give it a deceptive aroma of butter. • F

Some cheeses, such as Gorgonzola and blue, which may contain cow's milk—not goat's or sheep's milk—produce a yellow mixture, and this is bleached white with benzoyl peroxide, a highly inflammable chemical long used to bleach flour and fixed oils. In the cheese process, it destroys all traces of the milk's vitamin A content. (See COTTAGE CHEESE.) • F

CHERRIES

Eating lots of fresh cherries and cherry juice has been highly recommended in the treatment of gout and gouty arthritis. (Of course, one must avoid artificially colored or flavored cherries and the processed junk foods that often contain them.) • M

The leaves of wild cherries are poisonous. • E

CHOLESTEROL

Contrary to popular opinion, cholesterol problems do not always arise from eating cholesterol-yielding foods such as fatty meats, fried foods, and processed cheese. There is increasing evidence that many coronary artery disorders are not directly caused by dietary fat but rather by eating starches, together with, or im- • F

15

mediately following, the ingestion of meats, fish, or poultry. Desert the desserts. (Ask your gas-station friend what happens when a cupful of sugar is added to the gas tank. No go!) Another big reason for coronaries: very little or no physical exercise.

F • Good to take some vegetable oil daily. Its high content of unsaturated fatty acids greatly helps to liquefy the fats in the body and prevent their clogging the arteries.

CLOVES

M • Clove oil (from mashed cloves) is prescribed by many dentists as an effective quieter of throbbing nerves in a tooth that has lost its filling.

H • A few whole cloves in a small, porous, cloth bag help to keep moths out of the closet. Keep a bag in every closet and with stored linens and clothes.

COCONUT

F • To open a coconut, use a clean screwdriver to punch holes all the way through the three ridges (eyes) that appear on one end. Drain the liquid and enjoy a healthful drink. Place the coconut on a hard surface, pound heavily with a hammer to break the husk into pieces, and remove the inside meat with a sharp paring instrument.

F • Coconut oil is one of the very few vegetable oils high in cholesterol, so it should be eaten sparingly.

COFFEE

F • Crush dried eggshells and add to the coffeepot for an easy source of calcium. Also adds flavor.

F • Add a new taste to leftover coffee by adding a small stick of cinnamon to a potful of the warming liquid.

H • Save leftover coffee and tea during the summer months in ice-cube trays. Better than the usual ice cubes and they don't dilute the drinks.

COFFEE SUBSTITUTES

Some coffee substitutes are acorn shells or peanut shells, chick-peas, soybeans, rye, oats, barley, and chicory. The foods should be dried (in an oven or in sunlight) and roasted for an hour. The chicory root can be gathered in midsummer, dried, and thinly cut before roasting, or can be purchased cheaply—a 6-ounce box for not much more than 75¢. I have found that ½ to 3 ounces of prepared chicory, added to 1 pound of coffee, increases the yield by 30 percent, approximately 10 extra cups. Chicory can also be bought in tablet form, each tablet replacing 1 tablespoon of coffee in preparing 5 or 6 cups.

• F

COMPOSTING

Many of my organic-gardening friends obtain an abundance of free fertilizer from their garbage, from vegetable leftovers, grass and tree cuttings (and those of their noncomposting neighbors and friends), the refuse of supermarkets and restaurants, and composted material found in rich, wooded areas and brooksides, etc. When our herb club had a quarter-acre organic garden several years ago, certain members deposited many carloads of such wastes in the loving arms of the earth. No need to spray

• G

harmful chemical fertilizers and bug killers; no need to water that garden all summer long.

G • When you realize that one must love Mother Earth at all times, that from her comes our health, you'll start immediately to be kind to the soil, to replenish the nutrients you borrowed from the soil in last summer's produce that nourished you and your family.

G • All vegetable refuse belongs in your organic garden, either as an extra ingredient of the compost pile or as a mulch for your vegetable rows. Refuse can include rinds of fruit, corn cobs, peelings of potato, onion, pits, plate scrapings, etc. Place bones and meat castoffs, skin and entrails, at the bottom of the compost pit, 2 or 3 feet below the ground's surface. For compost, we cut up our refuse into small pieces. For mulch, place a flat stone over the minced items, and the worms will complete the fertilization of the soil.

G • Arrange for compost piles every 10 to 15 feet around the garden area. Alternate layers of refuse with layers of soil. Some people add lime. Books on organic gardening offer directions for faster decomposition.

G • In the fall, take several boxes of such rich soil indoors for the plants in your kitchen. If growing aromatic herbs, dilute 1 portion of compost with 2 parts of sand and mix well. To lessen the mineral deficiency of your garden soil, add a heavy layer of composted material to it and alternate a sprinkle, or very thin layer, of ground rock. Do this in the fall after harvesting your crop.

COOKING

F • Save your vegetables from drowning in hot water. The less water used, the less flavor and texture are lost, as well as water-soluble vitamins, minerals, and enzymes. Steaming your vegetables is best. Put a bought steamer inside a pot, or try fitting your colander or french-fryer. Put an inch or so of water in bottom, not letting the vegetable touch the water. The cover must fit well, to keep in the steam. Steam leafy vegetables until just wilted, others until tender.

18

Cook your vegetables at the lowest temperature possible; it helps • **F**
to keep vegetables whole and to maintain a maximum amount of
their nutrients.

Try using a double boiler on one heater instead of 2 or 3 separate • **F**
pots to cook 2 or 3 separate vegetables. Save heat, time, and
washing time later on. There's more heat at the bottom: cook
fresh vegetables there, leftover vegetables above. If you must boil
carrots or potatoes, use the bottom. Cook soup or stew there, too.
The top is also for heating rolls or steaming winter squash. Top
part is for steaming peas, beans, or squash, or for preparing a
sauce. Also use the upper boiler for small amounts of foods. In a
saucepan they'll dry out quickly but over hot water they will
retain their moisture.

Always cover the pot in which vegetables are cooking. This helps • **F**
to keep the natural color and flavor of vegetables, if not over-
cooked. Do avoid stirring the food. Stirring puts extra air into the
food, and air reduces the vitamin content.

Challenge: Try going one whole day (three meals) without eating • **F**
cooked foods.

COOKING UTENSILS

Aluminum cooking ware should be outlawed from every Amer- • **H**
ican kitchen. Rarely does the European chef permit any alumi-

num item in his kitchen. Aluminum leeches out the nutrients in foods. Cookbooks tell you to add either vinegar or lemon juice to whatever is cooking in your aluminum pot, to prevent it from turning dark, and that's enough reason not to use such a utensil. (See UNSAFE COOKING UTENSILS.)

H • Recommended: stainless steel, iron, enamel, and glassware (not necessarily in that order). Except for glass, these containers were always in my mother's and my aunts' kitchens. The quality of these utensils for keeping the heat even and gently transferring it to the food were well known and of prime importance to these good cooks. It is interesting to note that we import enameled iron pots, casseroles, and skillets from Denmark, Belgium, and France. (See UNSAFE COOKING UTENSILS.)

H • To remove hard-water rings from your stainless steel pans, soak a cloth with rubbing alcohol and apply it to the area.

H • Instead of scrubbing off the baked-on food particles from your electric frying pan or cooker, add hot water and a few drops of dishwashing liquid (detergent or soap) to the pan and warm it at a low temperature for a few minutes. Shut it off and allow the pan to cool before you wash and rinse it.

H • To quickly loosen burned food that's really stuck to enamelware or to a casserole dish, fill it with boiling water in which you dissolve a tablespoon of washing (soda carbonate) or baking soda (soda bicarbonate). Works fast.

H • Although you must never eat rhubarb leaves since they contain a harmful excess of oxalic acid, you may use them as a worthy cleaning agent for silver and for discolored aluminum pots, if you still use such cookware.

H • Flour sifter: Avoid washing to prevent flour lumps and rust. Keep in a bag when not in use. To clean it, use a large chicken feather or vegetable brush.

H • To prevent the bottom of a kettle from burning, keep two marbles in it at all times. They will rattle when more water is needed.

CO-OP

One way to beat the high cost of foods is to form your own food • F
co-op with several of your neighbors. A group of 10 families has
great buying power—not only with regard to price but also for
obtaining dried organic foods (cereals, grains, legumes, etc.) and
fresh, organically raised produce.

Once a centrally located place is decided upon—a home,
church vestry, and so on—the members meet once a week to
discuss policies, plans, and the buying and distributing of the
separate orders.

You will find owners of health food stores more often than
not anxious to cut their profit margin, to help food co-ops. Of
course, once you are organized into a working unit, you may
approach another co-op in your state or local area and make
terms for future purchases.

But by all means, contact your nearest health food store,* which
will gladly sell you bulk amounts of "dry goods" at wholesale
prices.

Here are the price differences (February 1973) between store-
bought produce (a) and our co-op's (b):

	a	b
apples	23¢ lb.	12¢ lb.
broccoli	48¢ bunch	37¢ bunch
cucumber	20¢ each	15¢ each
eggplant	39¢ each	19¢ each
green peppers	38¢ lb.	23¢ lb.
lettuce	38¢ head	30¢ head
onions	29¢ lb.	19¢ lb.
oranges	11¢ each	8¢ each
potatoes	12¢ lb.	7¢ lb.
spinach	38¢ pkg.	27¢ pkg.
squash (butternut)	22¢ lb.	18¢ lb.
tomatoes	38¢ lb.	31¢ lb.

---

* For example, the Erewhon Trading Company, 342 Newbury Street, Boston,
Massachusetts 02115, which is both a retail store and a wholesale supplier to
stores.

There is an overall saving of 35 to 40 percent on dried beans, lentils, and most other dry items.

Even books may be purchased at substantial savings: many publishers will sell a co-op a minimum of 25 books (assorted titles) at 33⅓ percent off. You will find the publishers' names and addresses in your favorite health-oriented books. Write for their latest catalog and discount schedule.

CORN

F • Freshness is a must! Corn from the garden to the pot would be ideal, because almost half the sugar is lost within 24 hours of picking time. Buy young corn, preferably at farm road stands. Select ears with bright green, tight-fitting husks and dark brown silk. If you are buying corn in the supermarket, purchase only enough for the next meal. Cook and eat corn as soon as bought. Reason: sugar content changes to starch quickly after picking, with consequent loss of flavor. To store corn, refrigerate in husks. There, the natural action of its juices is retarded. *One-third of vitamin C is lost too.*

F • Have you ever eaten freshly picked corn *not* cooked? Mmmmm. Cooked or not, chew, chew, chew very well so that the starch will be thoroughly digested.

F • To remove the kernels from fresh corn, place the ear in the hole of an angel food cake pan and press down firmly. Small to medium-sized ears fit the pan's hole; larger-sized ones can be held there and scored with a knife. My mother and aunts mounted corn on a large nail on a board to remove the kernels.

F • Leftover corn cut from the cob may be incorporated in an omelet, and in soups and stews. Or add the corn to a pancake batter.

F • Popcorn will pop better if you leave it in the freezer for a full 24 hours before using.

G • Save the corncobs. Instead of discarding them, break them up in small pieces, allow them to dry thoroughly (wet cobs tend to mold when placed in soil), and incorporate them in your garden. In the

22

winter, save the dried, chopped cobs in a box until spring gardening time.

Save the corn silk, too. Steep 1 teaspoon of dried silk in a cup of • **M**
hot water and use as a kidney remedy and for cystitis. Drink a
cupful of the infusion 4 times a day.

CORNMEAL

Always check your cornmeal for weevils, especially when you've • **F**
just arrived home with a package. If there is no sign of them, put
the meal in a double plastic bag, label, and refrigerate or store in
the freezer.

A dry shampoo comes in handy when you have the sniffles. • **C**
Old-fashioned cornmeal serves beautifully. Pour a little of the
powder on your hairbrush and brush vigorously—until every last
trace is removed. You will note how effectively the meal removes
dust particles, dandruff, and excess oil. Be sure to spread newspaper around you before using the powder.

Ordinary cornmeal can serve as a top-notch skin cleanser. • **C**
Prepare suds with a mild soap in water, wet a washcloth with the
suds and sprinkle the meal onto the cloth and thoroughly scrub
the face and neck. The gentle abrasive action, I understand,
removes dead outer tissue, cleans the pores, and refreshes the skin.

CORNSTARCH

H • A generation ago, cornstarch served young mothers as a dusting powder to absorb the child's excessive skin secretions; and grandmothers cleaned their furs by gently rubbing a little in with gentle pressure and shaking the fur thoroughly.

COTTAGE CHEESE

F • Here are two ways of making cottage cheese:
1. If you start with clabbered milk, apply *very low* heat to the container until the cheese separates. Strain the liquid (whey) out through cheesecloth and set it aside. What remains is cottage cheese. That watery part of the milk contains the sugar, minerals, and some protein and should be saved. Store both in refrigerator.
2. If you start with regular milk (certified raw, if possible), heat it in a double boiler and when warm, stir in small amounts of lemon juice—up to 1 tablespoonful. Keep at low heat and when curdling takes place, remove the container from the stove. Allow to set a few minutes, then strain through several layers of cheesecloth. (A muslin bag may also be used.)

F • The mineral-rich whey may be taken with apple juice or flavored with a citrus juice of your choice.

F • Whey may also be used as a skin and hair conditioner. Massage the face with it until the skin begins to brace. Let it stay on for 10 to 15 minutes and rinse with tepid water. In earlier days, whey was massaged into the hair before shampooing.

COUGH REMEDY

M • Need a cough remedy in a hurry? Mix 2 teaspoons of lemon juice in ½ to ⅔ cup of warm water and add enough honey to thicken. Take 1 or 2 teaspoonsful every hour as needed.(See also ANISE, CABBAGE, HONEY, IRISH MOSS, QUINCE, and THYME.)

CRANBERRIES

A healthful and satisfying food product is yielded when you use • **F**
your blender. Sweeten with honey. To improve the flavor, let the
mixture stand an hour or so before serving. Makes a good cold
relish and preserves its rich vitamin C content.

There are many ways to make cranberry sauce. Here are three • **F**
possibilities:

1. 1 cup cranberries
   ½ orange
   ½ cup honey or
   raw sugar

   Combine the berries and orange in a
   blender, remove and add honey. Stir
   thoroughly. Let stand 2 or 3 hours.
   Refrigerate.

2. 2 cups cranberries
   1 orange, cut in
   small pieces, or
   1 cup orange
   juice
   ¾ cup honey or
   raw sugar
   ½ tablespoon chopped
   walnuts

   Cook cranberries in enough hot water
   to prevent scorching and until all
   skins pop open. Remove from heat,
   mix in the orange, the honey, and
   nuts. Let stand several hours. Refrigerate.

3. 2 cups cranberries
   2 cups water
   1 cup honey or
   raw sugar

   Cook berries until the skins pop open,
   about 5 to 6 minutes. Bring to boil,
   add honey, and boil 2 minutes. Let
   stand several hours. Refrigerate.

In early colonial days, Yankee seamen used raw cranberries to • **F**
prevent scurvy just as their English contemporaries used limes.

The peculiar tartness and zest of the fruit are due to a combina- • **M**
tion of malic, citric, quinic, and benzoic acids, thus indicating a
decided antiseptic value in urinary infections. For that purpose
they're usually prepared as a jelly or sauce and even eaten raw.
They may also be served as a raw cranberry-apple relish or
crunch.

M • A long-time customer of mine greatly reduced the size of a huge, annoying mole positioned near the nose by keeping it moist with alternate applications of thin cranberry slices and a combination of cranberry juice and castor oil.

CREAM

F • Before beating heavy cream, make sure it is 1 or 2 days old. It will then beat more easily and produce a greater volume.

F • Substitute for whipped cream: blend one *ripe* banana with egg white(s) until the mixture becomes thick.

CREAM, SOURED

F • Always add a tablespoonful of sour cream to a serving of hot or cold beet, spinach, or sorrel soup. Helps counteract the oxalic acid content.

F • Sour cream sauce: incorporate your favorite finely ground or powdered herbs, and add a little beet liquid for color.

CUCUMBER

F • Cukes bought from local growers are generally not waxed, but most of those found in the supermarket are. To dewax this food (as well as green peppers and rutabagas), soak the food for 5 minutes in a quart of tap water containing 10 to 15 drops of liquid detergent. Then wash with 1 tablespoonful of herbal or brown vinegar. Rinse in fresh tap water and rub off with a towel. Do not soak in salted water.

G • Peel cucumber sparingly to retain nutrients under the peel.

M • And did you know that ground eggshells and diced potato scrapings are excellent nutrients for the cuke vines? Incorporate them in the soil around the plants.

F • This food has long been recognized as an excellent diuretic, and its juice, taken with the carrot's, helps to reduce the uric acid content that causes rheumatic ailments. The juice's high amount of potassium is said to help maintain blood pressure. It also enhances the activity of erepsin, a protein-digesting enzyme of the intestinal juice.

For face irritations: Cut a few *thin* slices of cuke. Soak a slice for a minute in a solution of equal parts of witch hazel and warm water, then apply. Massage the area four times a day. • **M**

Save the ends of cukes as a jiffy hand lotion. Either squeeze out a little juice as needed or pare ¼ inch of the vegetable and rub it onto chapped or irritated skin. The juice is an excellent application for chapped hands and roughness of the skin and is a good astringent. • **C**

Before retiring, wash face with cold water, then massage a little cucumber juice into aging areas of the face. • **C**

If your skin has unusually high color, apply one or more slices to the skin and eye area to cool and tone down the color. Leave on a few minutes, then wash with lemon juice, diluted with tepid water. • **C**

DATES

The date is a most nourishing food, high in vitamins A, B, D, and G, and especially the minerals of calcium, phosphorus, potassium, iron, sodium, copper, and magnesium. This superior food needs but one or two apricots, a banana (or other sweet fruit), and a teaspoonful of cottage cheese to make a lunch complete. • **F**

Instead of giving children the usual, harmful candies, chocolates, and worthless sweets, do offer them dates—if only to protect their health. • **F**

Dates have gentle laxative properties. For that purpose, five or six may be soaked in warm water until cool. They should be chewed well and followed by the remaining water. This should be done morning and night. • **M**

DIET

M • Almost every American adult over the age of 45 is now on some particular diet, most of which have been ordered by their doctors. Especially popular are salt-free, spice-free, low-carbohydrate, low-protein, fat-free, and sugar-free diets. Once you realize with what ailments these dieters are afflicted, you will utilize these diets as clues to how to avoid those diseases. Do this while you are still in good health.

I favor neither crash nor phony diets. If the ill are forbidden salted or spicy foods, sugars, starches, or heavily fatted foods, it makes sense to omit them from all diets. Also avoid all processed, bottled, packaged, and artificially made foods. For example, only the orange, not processed juice, provides *all* the nutrients.

E • A few dietary rules:
- Eat only when you're hungry and not by the clock.
- Chew foods thoroughly. Eat slowly and you'll digest the foods with greater ease.
- Avoid multicourse banquets.
- Simplify your meals: Eat fruits at one meal, vegetables at another. Protein and starch eaten together are difficult to digest.
- Drink no liquids with or at the end of the meal.
- Don't overeat. You'll overburden the organs and bring discomfort to the whole body.
- Skip the meal if you're nervous, overtired, excited, or ill at ease because of family or business problems.
- No eating between meals. Give the stomach a chance to do its work. A compromise: a few grapes or one fresh apricot, or a sip of fruit juice.
- Fruits are golden in the morning, but lead at night.
- Eat none of the four whites: sugar, salt, vinegar, and starch, and foods which contain them.
- Avoid TV snacks and drinks and the Dagwood-type foods after suppertime.
- Try to abandon as many artificially made foods as possible—processed, boxed, packaged, canned, frozen, and so on.

On your Sabbath day—Tuesday, Friday, Saturday, or Sunday—try fasting and resting; drink only diluted fruit juices until suppertime. Then have a *small* vegetable salad but chew every morsel thoroughly.

DILL

Since biblical days, dill has been used as a seasoner of foods and a medicinal remedy. In the past five or six centuries, the herb has been used to flavor fruits, roots, cucumbers, fish and meat, soups, beans, and starchy vegetables. And the herbalists of the seventeenth and eighteenth centuries used the seeds to eliminate the disease-causing "raw and viscous humors," especially when indicated in stomach or intestinal disorders.

Dill is easily grown on the windowsill garden. Be sure to dilute the soil with ⅓ part of sand. Plant only a few seeds at a time in a flower (nonplastic) pot. When the seedlings are 5 to 6 inches high, they may be cut for table use. Use the minced tops to flavor cottage or creamed cheese, soup, and omelets.

One of my pet remedies for colic in infants has been to steep ⅛ teaspoonful each of dill, anise, and catnip or fennel in a cup of hot water. Give from a tablespoon to ½ a bottle of the strained liquid every 2 hours in a nursing bottle.

DRIED FRUIT

Most boxed, dried fruits on supermarket shelves have been treated with chemicals and preservatives: raisins and apricots with sulfur dioxide, mixed fruits with sulfur dioxide and potassium sorbate, prunes with potassium sorbate, and pitted prunes with sorbic acid. (Sorbic acid was originally obtained from unripe mountain ash fruits. It and its potassium salt are now *sin*-thetically made and used principally as a fungicide and food preservative.)

Dried fruits like apples, apricots, peaches, nectarines, and pears undergo the sulfur-dioxide treatment not only to prevent darkening while drying; the process is also said to prevent fermentation and decay and to protect the fruits from insects and their larvae. But the sulfuring process also makes the fruits' texture less porous and nullifies or destroys their desired alkalinity. However, sulfured fruits may be consumed if, first, they are soaked for one hour in cold water. Repeat the procedure each time you wish to eat these dried fruits.

F • The Federal Food and Drug Administration requires the label to declare which chemicals are used for artificial flavoring, artificial coloring, and preserving. Every man-made chemical has its "maximum level of use" and tolerance.

F • Organically grown fruits are sun-dried and unsulfured and may be found in health food stores. They may cost slightly more but are well worth it. Cover them with water and completely soften the fruit. The syrup that remains after the soaking makes a delicious drink.

DRINKING WITH MEALS

F • Try to avoid the harmful habit of drinking liquids immediately before, during, or directly after a meal. This includes water, soda pop, and milk during the meal, and tea or coffee following the meal. Its OK to take water, fruit, or vegetable juice a half hour before or between meals. If you're that thirsty during a meal, eliminate the salt and spices and the foods with which they're "seasoned"—the condiments, pickles, relishes, and other artificial stimulants of thirst. Chew your foods well, eat slowly, and you'll need no liquid to wash them down. Yet a thick bean or pea soup with other vegetables added is acceptable, if taken without bread or crackers.

F • A drink between meals is acceptable: try spring or distilled water—the latter tastes like freshly fallen rainwater—or the freshly expressed juice of fruits or vegetables. A mineral broth: an infusion of carrot and beet greens, the leaves of parsley, celery, and peas. A refreshing tea: mint, catnip, thyme, rose leaves. Chamomile is aromatic and quickly counteracts gas and bilious attacks.

F • To reach your proverbial "eight glasses of water a day," eat a large salad of vegetables for supper and far more fresh, uncooked fruits and vegetables during the day. Whenever you think vegetable or fruit juice, eat the vegetable or fruit itself instead. But an occasional freshly expressed juice should be sipped slowly and swished in the mouth before swallowing—*not* gulped down hastily. "Only man and duck drink at meals," say my health-minded friends. "It may be right for the duck but it is wrong for man."

Children who copy their parents' habit of drinking at mealtime usually take to such foods as require the least effort to eat—mushy-soft and sweet foods—which too often lead to more dental and health decay. • **F**

Cold or iced water, tea, or coffee will chill the stomach, delaying the digestive process. Iced drinks in the summertime are often responsible for stomach and bowel complaints. Ordinarily, drinking water should be at tap temperature. Hot drinks injure the delicate mucous linings of the alimentary system. • **M**

EGGS

Buy only for one week's needs. • **F**

Washing eggs before storing them removes a natural protective • **F**
coating that keeps air and assorted odors from entering the shell.

Acceptable and fresh: the white should appear quite jelly-like and • **F**
the yolk unblemished and spherical. An older egg has a more liquid white and a yolk that is flat on top.

Eggs stored with their broad end up will yield fewer broken yolks. • **F**

F • Refrigerating hard-boiled eggs? Write H.B. on them. Prevents accidents.

F • The quality of brown and white eggs is the same. (In some localities, you pay more for brown eggs; in some, more for white eggs.)

F • Freeze any unused yolks that will not be needed in a day or so. They will come in handy for a future sponge cake.

F • Eggs cook better if they are not cold. Let them remain at room temperature before using, until the chill has gone.

F • Egg whites yield a larger whipped volume and whip better if they're at room temperature.

F • Use leftover yolks when making fudge, cakes, custard, and cream filling. They are a necessary ingredient, together with sherry, for a delicious zabaglione dessert.

F • Prepare an omelet with leftover vegetables, plus chopped onion, green pepper, and celery leaves, and season with basil or oregano.

F • Having difficulty separating eggs? Break the egg into a funnel over a small glass. The yolk remains in the funnel while the whites will pass through.

F • Do you know the trick about retrieving bits of shell that have fallen in with the egg? Don't try to get them out with spoon or fork—too slippery. Use the eggshell.

F • Percolate coffee with eggshells or whole yolk to add flavor and nourishment.

G • Dry and powdered eggshells are excellent food for your rose-bushes and other garden flowers and plants. Be sure to apply them a few inches below the surface of soil.

M • Use the dried shells of uncooked eggs as an extra source of calcium. Powdered or ground finely, they may be taken along with a drink of your choice, and you have a superb, most assimilable form of calcium at no charge.

Use an egg white with 3 ounces of linseed oil as an application for a scald or recent burn.   • **M**

Is that egg a hard-cooked one or an uncooked one? A raw egg won't spin fast, while a hard-cooked one will spin around like a top.   • **H**

A broken or dropped egg? Remove contents from shell into a dish and cover tightly. Refrigerate. Salvaged egg may be used as a shampoo–hair conditioner. Soap-wash the hair, rinse, and work into the scalp a well-beaten egg. Allow to remain a few minutes and rinse well twice.   • **C**

Turn that egg white of the broken egg into a facial, a beauty treatment, and a skin toner. Wash the face with tepid water and soap. Remove the egg white from the refrigerator, beat it slightly, and smear it on the face. Or pat it on with absorbent cotton. Allow it to dry and apply another coating. In 15 to 20 minutes, rinse with tepid water and rub in enough avocado or cold cream to offset any drying effect. Your skin will feel baby soft, look fresh and clean, and feel grand.   • **C**

Variation: Beat the white of one egg until stiff and blend in a teaspoonful of honey. Smooth the mixture over the surface of the skin with a pad of cotton or cloth and allow to stay for 15 to 20 minutes. Rinse first with a lemon-juice-and-tepid-water mixture and then with cold water. Two applications a week will greatly improve skin blemishes, acne, blackheads, and so on.   • **C**

ENTERTAINING CHILDREN

When parents are in the kitchen, toddlers want to be there, too, and if you put just a little effort into entertaining them, they will not be in your way. For instance: • **E**

If you have extra drawer space, keep a low drawer full of your children's toys. Or keep a boxful in the kitchen.

A junk drawer will fascinate them, one where you throw odds and ends; loose, small toys; and kitchen equipment that is not sharp,

such as measuring spoons, spatulas, garlic press, plastic utensils, wooden spoons, and so on.

Keep your canned goods on low shelves and let your children stack them. Most toddlers know how—somehow—to keep them from falling on bare feet.

A box of cornmeal, plus spoons for digging, makes an excellent sandbox.

Smear Vaseline on a cookie tray and let them fingerpaint. Food coloring may be added. Easily cleaned.

Save cereal and cracker boxes and let the kids stack them and/or glue them together.

Kids can glue macaroni to cardboard. Makes great bumpy designs.

Mix some liquid soap (not dangerous detergents—read the label!) with water and let them blow bubbles with straws, either on the floor or at the kitchen table. Large cake pans will catch the overflow.

Drape a long cloth over the kitchen table and let the children hide under it. It will be a house, a fire station, a tent, a cave. . . .

FASTING

These past few years, had you asked the members of my herb-study classes for one of their best remedies for sudden or temporary illness—headache, stomachache, or nausea, a cold or cough, etc.—the invariable answer would have amazed you: "Go to bed for a day or two and don't eat. Drink tepid herb teas three or four times a day."

With a grandfather as strict as he was kind, I had to be an apt student. He was Thoreauvian: "Live within the laws of Nature and you'll live a healthful, simple, worryless, long life." Another of his pet remarks: "Observe the habits of animals—your dog and cat, since we are all animals. When they are sick, they throw up and eat no more until they're fully recovered." And when one of our family fell ill with fever or stomach distress, no physician was called—who could afford the $1 fee? The patient was put right to bed, permitted no eating "until further notice," but given a brew of "bitters" as often as possible until emesis occurred. A whole day's rest-fast completed, he was given weak mint or catnip tea, and for supper, thinned chicken broth. Skipping a few meals meant no great hardship, and the body would be in far better condition.

When my cat or dog was sick, their favorite remedy was to chew grass and witchgrass respectively, and, having vomited thoroughly, to disappear for a few days. They ate no solid food, took only an occasional drop of water and preferred to lie in a warm or sunny place. They returned as chipper as ever. Grandfather was right, as usual. A short fast, I was to discover, is one of the oldest remedial methods by which man and animals provide the entire body, and thus every organ and system (e.g., nerves and heart) with complete rest.

For the past 20 years, I have fasted the first three days of every month, and when overtired or in need of introspection, I take a 5-day fast, with weak herb tea or well-diluted grape juice as my only "food." In January 1973, I fasted for 16 days. Nothing unusual. Others have fasted 40 to 60 days and more; but a fast over 5 days must be supervised by a qualified hygienic-practitioner.

Fasting is no sure cureall; it is the first step in detoxifying the system, in reconditioning the kidneys or alimentary process. This healing process is for sick and well. Fasting is but one of the spokes of my "health wheel"; it is as important as foods, organic gardening, exercise, sleep, and other "spokes." The practice is much discussed in the Bible. Moses, Elijah, and Jesus (and presumably many others) fasted 40 days, and such abstinence produced in them greater and clearer thinking power.

The neophyte faster may use the Sabbath day—that "holy [healing] day of rest" may be Friday, Saturday, or Sunday—to take leave of all physical work. But he or she must rest in bed or on a couch, eating no solid food except for sips of water when thirsty. What an excellent way to catch up on one's reading. The faster should select a sunny and well-aired room, there to relax, rest, sleep, and think (meditate) clearly and positively. The one-day-a-week fast continues for one or two months and becomes a two-day, bed-rest fast for a few weeks, and that practice leads up to a monthly three-day fast. On the second day, the usual "pangs of hunger" are greatly diminished, although the habitual drinker or smoker may experience several temporary withdrawal symptoms—mild headaches or nausea. Try it: you'll experience one of nature's wonderful ways of healing.

FENNEL

F • Fennel has an old reputation for slenderizing and should for this reason become more and more popular in this overweight nation. It is a thrifty food to grow because you can eat its several parts: the stalk and head like celery, the leaves in salad and sauce for fish, and the seeds as flavoring for spaghetti, chicken, sausage, and meat. Or simmer fennel seeds to make a tea.

M • Remember, it's "fennel in the kennel," and if your dog is tortured by insects or has been spreading his fleas around, you might copy my flea remedy. Mix together 3 ounces of powdered "insect

flowers" (pyrethrum) and fennel, and 1 of powdered sassafras powder.

FIGS

Besides being a delicious food, figs are also medicinally useful. Cut in half and steeped for 2 or 3 minutes in hot water, the fig is good for applying to boils or abscesses.

• **M**

The juice gotten by soaking 2 or 3 figs is a remedy for a simple sore throat or cough, for digestive disturbances, and for temporary constipation.

• **M**

FINES HERBES

If your cookbook mentions *fines herbes,* what is meant is a blend of herbs, preferably fresh, which may include minced basil, chervil, chives, marjoram, parsley, rosemary, thyme, and tarragon. The four traditional *fines herbes* are chervil, parsley, tarragon, and chives.

• **F**

FIRE EXTINGUISHERS

A small fire extinguisher is not only an excellent investment for home and business alike; it is an extra insurance policy as well. A small-sized one is suitable for the kitchen and for the cellar workshop, and its mode of operation can and should be taught to all teenagers, parents, and grandparents. The label of our com-

• **H**

37

mercial (dry chemical) fire extinguisher states that it "extinguishes grease, oil, gasoline, and electrical fires." Be sure yours has the UL (Underwriters' Laboratories, Inc.) "seal of approval." We keep one on the cellar stairs for use in the first floor and cellar; another on the second floor for that area and the attic.

H • For a handy homemade fire extinguisher, keep a coffee can of either salt or bicarbonate of soda near your stove.

H • Another homemade fire extinguisher, suggested by a Vermont fireman, is to put in a special faucet under your kitchen sink and attach a hose to it.

H • I've been told of someone putting firecrackers into his walls as he built his home, to act as fire alarms. I do not know if they become soggy and useless after a while.

FISH

F • To help avoid the odor of fried fish that hangs in the air after it is cooked, set the fish in a little vinegar (or lemon juice) and herbs for 15 to 20 minutes before covering with meal and frying.

F • Leftover fish is good made into chowder with added parsley, onion, and leftover vegetables.

H • To remove fish odor from your hands, wash them with either a solution of sodium bicarbonate (a tablespoonful to a quart of warm water) or with herb (or brown) vinegar, or rub them with a thin slice of lemon. Or you may squeeze the juice from two slices of lemon into tepid water and then rinse your hands.

FIRST AID

ANTIDOTES:

M • One should be familiar with antidotes for all kinds of poisoning. The Universal Antidote is especially helpful: two parts powdered burnt toast (or activated charcoal), one part milk of magnesia, one part strong tea. The dosage is 2 to 4 teaspoonfuls in water or milk taken hourly 3 to 4 times to neutralize the poison. Vomiting

38

should be induced as soon as possible. This preparation is intended for unknown poisons, acids, drugs, and dangerous plants.

Has your child swallowed disinfectant, detergent, rubbing alcohol, or bleach? Have the child slowly drink two glasses of milk and wait a few minutes. Then give a teaspoonful of syrup of ipecac, or enough to cause vomiting. For furniture polish, do as above. Follow with 2 ounces (4 tablespoons) of vegetable oil.

A remedy for dust, smoke, or fumes is to put 2 drops of castor oil in each eye.

BEESTINGS:

An 1840 antidote for beestings: "Bind on the place a thick plaster • **M** [paste] of saleratus [soda bicarbonate] moistened; it will soon expend the Venom."

BURNS:

Many different things will help the pain of burns: cold water; • **M** milk and egg white; egg white and 3 ounces of linseed oil; a thin paste of bicarbonate of soda in cold milk or vinegar; cold witch hazel extract; butter; honey; vegetable oils; vanilla extract; a thin slice of potato; lanolin.

M • *INSECT BITES:*

Dissolve a heaping teaspoonful of sodium bicarbonate in vinegar and use with an equal part of cold witch hazel. Or saturate a piece of cotton with household ammonia and press it on the sting for a few minutes.

M • *POISON IVY:*

Make a thick solution of brown washing soap in hot water. Apply as warm as possible every hour for 4 or 5 hours. If you know you have been exposed to poison ivy, take the immediate precaution of washing the exposed area with this brown soap. Most likely, you will thereby prevent a serious rash.

FLOWERS

G • Cut flowers last longer if the leaves below the water level are removed. Also, the water will stay fresher.

G • To make your cut flowers last longer, place them in a solution of tea, diluted 1 part tea to 4–6 parts water.

G • To prevent colorful flowers from fading for weeks, cut the stems off about ¾ inch and let them stand in a weak solution of glycerin, one teaspoon to 7–8 ounces of water.

G • Preparing a flower arrangement? Omit sweet peas. They have a devastating, wilting effect on other flowers.

G • A novel effect: Add a few drops of food coloring to your clear glass flower bowls. To make the stems appear less conspicuous, add a few drops of green food coloring.

FROZEN FOODS

F • Buy your frozens last—just before leaving the store—and have them packed in an insulated bag. Once home, place them in the freezer immediately.

F • These foods may be frozen: freshly baked bread, parsley, dill and other herbs, sauce for pasta, and soup. Unlike beef, fowl (chicken, turkey, squab, and pheasant) will not deteriorate in the freezer.

Cook frozen vegetables covered and at a low heat. If label says to • **F** use liquid, use canned vegetable juice, or a leftover juice, or chicken broth, although the frost in frozen vegetables usually offers enough water for the preparation.

Storing leftover chicken or beef stock? Freeze them in ice-cube • **F** trays. Remove the cubes and store in plastic bags in the freezer. Label. Remove as needed.

Frozen food in damaged containers? Don't buy. Tell the store • **E** manager.

FRUIT

Fresh fruits lose too much of their nutrients when soaked even in • **F** cold water.

Berries, grapes, and cherries may be refrigerated unwashed and • **F** unstemmed. Just before using, wash them quickly with cold water.

Eat all melons (musk, cantaloupe, watermelon) at room temper- • **F** ature. Remove from refrigerator and leave on the table overnight, or at least several hours before eating. Then all the fruit's taste will be available.

Season your stewing fruits with anise, cardamon, cinnamon, or • **F** rosemary.

Do your own canning or dehydrating? When fruits are plentiful • **F** or when it is near the end of the growing season, inquire (from your local County Extension Service) about a surplus of fresh, locally grown produce. Arrange to buy (alone or in cooperation with several friends or club members) a large quantity of your favorite vegetables and tree-maturing fruits and preserve them by whichever way is best for you.

Making children's beanbags? Save peach and plum seeds and • **E** cherry pits, wash and dry them, and fill the bags. They are lightweight and easy to use.

G

GARGLE

M • A quickie gargle: Steep a big pinch of sage and a small cinnamon stick in hot water for 20 minutes, stir and strain, and gargle warm every ¼ to ½ hour as needed. You can also include black currants in this recipe.

M • And a quickie halitosis remedy: Steep ⅓ teaspoon each mint, rosemary, and anise or fennel seed in a covered cup of hot water for 10 minutes. Stir and strain. Rinse the mouth or use as a gargle as often as necessary. Do sip a little occasionally, for the problem may be a digestive one.

GARLIC

F • When using a whole clove in a soup or stew or sauce, stick a toothpick through it. This helps to avoid losing the garlic while it is cooking with the food.

F • The pressed juice and the diced clove of garlic are suitable for salad dressing and a thin application of the juice may be added to a vegetable plate.

G • Garlic bulbs should be used sparingly—please see ONION. They can, however, safely be sprouted and cut for use. They need well-watered, sandy soil, and the 8- to 10-inch leaves may later be cut for use. Garlic sprouts will grow anywhere in your kitchen.

H • Pressed garlic yields a lot more flavor to food than diced garlic. If you are dissatisfied with your garlic press, try the kind that has a circular top which fits snugly into a circular holder, sometimes imported from France or Switzerland.

GINGER

For the quick relief of menstrual cramps: Mix ¼ teaspoon powdered ginger and ⅛ teaspoon each of powdered cloves and cinnamon in ½ cup of warm wine (20 percent alcohol). Allow to infuse for 1 hour but stir the mixture 2 or 3 times. Take 2 to 3 tablespoons in ½ cupful warm water every hour or two as needed.

• **M**

GLASS

To make your glassware sparkle, add a few drops of household ammonia to the dishwater.

• **H**

To pick up broken glass, wet a cloth, newspaper, paper towel, facial tissue, or absorbent cotton and press over the fragments. Deposit in the garbage can.

• **H**

Glasses or babies' bottles that have held milk should first be rinsed in cold water before washing. Hot water will cause milk to stick to the glass.

• **H**

GRAINS

Whole grains have been used since time immemorial and are being used more and more today, as a source of nutrients and as an anti inflationary weapon. They may be used whole, sprouted, and stone-ground to prepare a coarsely ground cereal or a finely ground flour. The ground and unground seeds are used, as they were centuries ago, in bread and crackers, as a mush for morning meals, and in soups and stews.

• **F**

When grains go through commercial milling, they lose most of their life-sustaining elements—vitamins, germ, enzyme factors, and 50 to 85 percent of the essential minerals. Milling eliminates:

• **F**

gluten	sulfur	zinc
phosphorus	silicon	copper
calcium	iron	magnesium

cobalt	folic acid	thiamine
potassium	biotin	riboflavin
iodine	inositol	niacin
manganese	vitamin B$_6$	
pantothenic acid	vitamin E	

Present-day milling of wheat uses steel rollers that permit the germ to go through intact and later to be sifted out of the flour. When stone grinders were formerly used, the wheat germ was pulverized with the entire seed. This makes wheat germ especially rich in minerals such as iron, and vitamins A, B complex, C, and E. A half-cup of wheat germ offers about 24 grams of protein, as opposed to 3 grams in a heaping cupful of processed cold cereal, if you use raw instead of roasted wheat germ.

Today only starch and low-grade protein remain from the milling of wheat, and they are the chief ingredients of most white flour products, such as dry cereals, macaroni, spaghetti, and bread. The usual white breads are prepared with nutritionally worthless white flour but "enriched" with 30 different chemical additives. No matter what you pay for white bread, it's a needless waste of money and health. The same thing applies to polished white rice; the only nutrient left after the milling is the poor starch—and that's way out in left field.

F • For the sake of your health and pocketbook, eat no boxed or man-made foodless cereals so highly advertised on TV. (Would the farmer ever feed them to his cattle? No more than he'd feed corn flakes to his pigs or chickens. They'd die on that diet but thrive on the original corn.) Do eat unpolished or nondegerminated grains; they're the best nutritionally.

F • Millet (Pennisetum species) is very rich in protein matter, 15 out of the 22 amino acids, having more than oats have. In foxtail millet, a common weed, 10 of them exist in high amounts. Millet and sunflower are the least acid-forming of all seeds and grains; the latter is an excellent source of the essential phosphatides (lecithin, cephalin, etc.), and especially the unsaturated fatty acid vitamin F. The most acid-forming, and therefore the least desirable, are whole oats, whole rye, and whole wheat.

44

Grains are best taken with green (salad) vegetables and, being • **F**
acid-forming foods, as are peanuts, chestnuts, bread, potatoes,
and squash, must *not* be consumed before or with fruits.

A COMPARISON BETWEEN THE VITAMIN AND MINERAL COMPOSITION OF • **E**
GRAINS BASED ON AMOUNT PER 100 GRAMS OF FOOD:

	Protein Gm.	Calcium Mg.	—Phosphorus— Mg.	Iron— Mg.	Thiamin— Mg.	Riboflavin— Mg.	Niacin Mg.
Buckwheat							
(Dark flour)	11.7	33	347	2.8	.58	.15	2.9
(White flour)	6.4	11	88	1.0	.08	.04	.4
Oatmeal (dry)	14.2	53	405	4.5	.60	.14	1.0
(cooked)	2.3	9	67	0.7	.10	.02	0.2
Rice							
(raw brown)	7.5	39	303	2.0	.32	.05	4.6
(wild, raw)	14.1	19	339	—	.45	.63	6.2
Rye							
(whole grain)	12.1	38	376	3.7	.43	.22	1.6
(light flour)	9.4	22	185	1.1	.15	.12	.6
(dark flour)	16.3	54	536	4.5	.61	.22	2.7
Wheat							
(whole grain)	14.0	36	383	3.1	.57	.12	4.3
(all-purpose flour)	10.5	16	87	0.8	.06	.05	.9

GRAPEFRUIT

To a chilled, halved grapefruit, add a topping of cooked cran- • **F**
berries and a thin sprinkle of mint leaves.

Or add sections of the fruit to spread lettuce leaves, and center • **F**
with 2 tablespoons of cottage cheese.

The canned juice too sharp? Drain off into a jar and adjust the • **F**
taste with orange juice or a little honey.

GREEN BEANS

F • Fresh beans snap apart crisply when broken between the fingers.

F • Cold leftovers:
  · cut into small pieces or slit lengthwise and put into a vegetable salad. Season with a dash of basil or other herb vinegar, or French dressing.
  · add to a side dish containing sliced onion, parsley or chives, and chervil.
  · blend with French or Russian dressing, chill 15 to 20 minutes and add to a tossed salad.
  · steep in herb vinegar for one hour before serving.

F • Save the bean pot liquor. Use it in soup and stew, to thin blended vegetables, or with other leftover vegetable juices.

GREENS

F • Did you know that the nutrient greens of celery may be served in vegetable salad or incorporated in a soup or stew? That beet tops are a good solo steamed? That the leaves and flowering tops of radish may be steamed and so served?

F • Thoroughly dried tops of carrots, when finely ground and sifted, make a good "salt substitute."

G • Remember: All vegetable refuse—to the garbage pail, no; to the compost pile or garden, yes.

GROUND SPICES AND HERBS

F • A coffee mill will either coarsely grind spices, herbs, grains, and vegetable seeds, or will powder them quite finely. Powder the seasonings only as needed. They lose their aroma quickly when exposed to the air.

F • When individual herbs and spices are nearing their end, powder them via a coffee or meat grinder. If you add a little turmeric, you have your own curry powder.

HAND AND FACE LOTION

Add to ½ cup of strained unseasoned or nonfruit jelly made from • **C**
Irish moss about 1 tablespoonful of cucumber juice, and the
mixture becomes a splendid hand or face lotion for rough or
chapped skin.

Or when 2 teaspoonsful of honey and 1 of lemon juice are mixed • **M**
into the plain jelly, this item is not only a good skin lotion but as
good a cough syrup as ever you had.

HEADACHE

Why use drugs that could be dangerous? Do place a cold com- • **M**
press of witch hazel over the forehead. (See WITCH HAZEL.)

A white-coated tongue often indicates that your headache is • **M**
caused by an upset stomach. Try some sage tea made by steeping
a leaf in water for a few minutes.

HERBS

Seasoning herbs: A tablespoon of a fresh (garden) herb equals a • **F**
teaspoonful of the recently dried and ground. (Always note the
date of purchase of all dried herbs and spices on the label.)

To get the best of the delicate flavor of herbs, put them into the • **F**
preparation only in the last few minutes of cooking. Prolonged
cooking accounts for any unaromatic or bitter taste from herbs.

To season a soup or stew, immerse a cheesecloth bag containing • **F**
suitable herbs. Thus, no need for later straining.

Coarsely ground herbs are for sauces and mayonnaise and for • **F**
salad dressings and spreads. Finely powdered herbs are for salt
substitutes (herb powders).

47

F • Soup seasoning requires a variety of herbs. A soup bag: more (a teaspoon) of marjoram, dill, parsley, basil, and thyme, and far less (¼ teaspoon) of sage, savory, oregano, and rosemary.

F • Herb oils are easily prepared. Divide a pint of vegetable oil in four 4-ounce sections. Put into clean, dried glass jars (we use empty preserve glasses of uniform size). To each 4 ounces, add ½ to ⅔ teaspoon of herbs of your choice. Place on warm stove or radiator or oil burner for several days. Strain before using. Label the ingredients.

F • If you do not grow your own herbs (why not?), purchase your herbs preferably from an herb grower. All seasonings bought at a market should be purchased in small quantities and examined for freshness and taste. Be sure to put date of purchase on each package.

F • Before using aromatic seeds (caraway, anise, and so on) as seasoners, grind them coarsely and only enough for a given recipe. Any excess should be bottled and stored in a cool place or refrigerated. (See BOUQUET GARNI and FINES HERBES.)

F • *SOME HERBAL COOKING SUGGESTIONS:*

FRUITS AND VEGETABLES

Apples: anise, caraway, dill, and mint.
Beans: basil, dill, sage, and savory.
Beets: fennel, dill, and thyme.
Carrots: fennel, dill, and thyme.
Pears: mint, lemon balm.
Peas: basil, savory, and mint.
Tomatoes: basil, oregano, savory.
Turnips: dill, fennel, sage, tarragon.

SOUPS

Vegetable: parsley, marjoram, oregano, savory, basil, dill (herb), thyme, sage.
Chicken: basil, dill, marjoram, rosemary, tarragon, saffron.

48

Chowder: thyme, dill, basil, sage, savory, tarragon.

Consommé: parsley, savory, tarragon, dill, marjoram.

Onion: basil, oregano, thyme, marjoram.

Pea: savory, thyme, mint, dill, basil.

Soups of beans, peas, or vegetables: Add 2 teaspoons of basil or savory vinegar (1 teaspoonful of each) to a serving for six— near the end of the cooking.

SALADS

Cottage cheese salad: vegetables plus parsley and chervil, seasoned with vegetable oil, a little lemon juice or herb vinegar, and dill, cumin, marjoram, or thyme.

Danish cottage cheese: a heaping teaspoonful of ground sage stirred into a cup of heavy or sour cream. Refrigerate overnight. Mix with the cheese.

Tomato salad: Takes a little ground basil or oregano. Either herb can be used for the dressing.

EGGS

With eggs: try ½ teaspoonful each of parsley, thyme, and/or basil.

MEATS

With meats: sage, basil, mint, and savory.

A jiffy basting solution: Equal parts of wine and herb vinegar (or lemon juice) and a sprinkle of your favorite herbs.

With lamb chops: Brush each chop with your favorite herb vinegar and add a little of either marjoram or mint. Let stand an hour. Rub with vegetable oil and broil.

STEWS

With stew: marjoram, sage, parsley, grated lemon rind, celery seed, savory, and thyme.

Add to chicken stew (about 1½ pints): ⅓ to ¼ teaspoonful oregano. Heat and stir occasionally.

SARDINES

To serve: strain off the excess oil before sprinkling a teaspoonful of tarragon vinegar over the fish.

STUFFING

Instead of sage use equal parts of basil, savory, thyme, and dried lemon peel.

FISH SAUCE

Use herbs (coarsely ground) listed above under chowder. Add flavorings before cooking the sauce.

OYSTER STEW

Celery seed, dill seed, and others of your choice listed under chowder.

BAKED POTATO

Before baking: push two or three caraway seeds to the center. Or mix a little saffron butter in just before eating.

POTATO SALAD

Try this: a meager sprinkle of powdered dill or cumin seed.

MASHED POTATOES

If mashed potatoes are in the making: beat in basil vinegar (approximately ½ teaspoon) until the desired flavor is reached.

BUTTER SAUCE

Good for mushrooms and artichokes: into melted butter stir a little tarragon vinegar.

50

SPINACH

In a vegetable salad: spinach becomes an especially welcome
ingredient if preseasoned with a little marjoram or rosemary
vinegar.

GREENS

When serving cooked greens: blend 2 tablespoonsful each of basil
vinegar and garlic vinegar, and 4 tablespoonsful vegetable oil
and pour over the vegetables. Good for beet and dandelion
greens, broccoli, and Brussels sprouts.

COLESLAW

Try a dash of celery seeds (either whole or ground).

Use your empty sunshiny windowsills to grow your own herbs.
This feature adds glamour to your kitchen and is an excellent
conversation piece. You can easily grow dill, chives, garlic, on-
ions, nasturtiums, parsley, scallions, shallots, and watercress.
Sometimes mint.
• G

Use poor sandy soil for growing watercress, parsley, the onion
family, and nasturtiums. Nasturtiums in good soil will yield a lot
of foliage, far less taste, and a minimum of blossoms (which, by
the way, are edible).
• G

G • Parsley seeds have to be soaked in warm water for a day before planting.

See also DILL, MINT, ONION (for onions, garlic, chives, scallions, and shallots).

G • A large supply of freshly dried herbs should be bottled and stored in a cool place or refrigerated.

DRYING HERBS

G • To dry herbs, tie the stems and hang them upside down near the ceiling of a warm and well-ventilated room. An attic is good, or a cellar. Don't bunch them tightly or crowd them together.

HERB TEA

M • My grandfather's pet remedy was an herb tea ("bitters") which always awaited my sisters and myself (and I presume, my parents and my live-in aunts) for the slightest ailment. That strange-tasting tea was brewed with yarrow, boneset, dandelion, and of course sage. (See TEA for recipes.)

HONEY

F • Do try to use it instead of the harmful white or brown sugar.

F • When honey is used as a sugar replacement in a cake (or other) recipe, reduce the liquid called for by ¼ cup for each cup of honey used.

F • The granules that form in a jar of honey will reliquefy if the jar is placed in a pan of warm water.

M • Honey has a very interesting property, it absorbs moisture. From this, two uses follow. The first is germ-killing, when used as a dressing for burns and scalds. Bacteria are deprived of water and cannot live. The second use is as an aid in keeping a child dry at night. A teaspoonful given at bedtime will attract and hold fluid.

M • As a cough syrup, honey may be taken alone or added to a freshly prepared lemon tea (juice of two slices in ½ cup warm water). Sip slowly 1 teaspoonful every hour, as needed.

Honey was much used by the women of ancient Greece to moisten • C and heal skin irritations. A small amount was rubbed into the hands and legs in the early morning and midafternoon. This treatment, advised Hippocrates, would relieve discomforting or undesirable chapping and redness. Moisten the face with tepid water and apply a thin coating of slightly warmed pure honey. Also, try a blend of egg white, warm honey, and dry skim milk.

HORSERADISH

This is a harsh spice and should be used in small quantities. • F

Horseradish sauce, an easy-to-fix: Into ½ cup heavy cream (or • F thick sour cream), blend 3 tablespoonsful prepared horseradish and 1 teaspoonful each of lemon juice and ground rind. (Use a minimum of the sauce and of this harsh spice in general.)

HOUSE PLANTS

Forewarned is forearmed. Close to 100 plants grown in American • G gardens and houses are dangerous. If your table setting holds any lobelias taken from the garden or nearby pond edge, be sure to keep them away from inquisitive children. Should they take any part of the plant's milky juice or even nibble the stem, they may be affected by a painful contraction of the throat, accompanied or followed by extreme nausea.

Eating poinsettia leaves has proven fatal to children. • G

Narcissus blooms cause many people to suffer feverish colds, • G rhinitis, and so on.

Jimsonweed, foxglove, and lily of the valley should never be kept • G in a house with young children. Jimsonweed has dangerous narcotic-like properties; dried foxglove leaves and lily of the valley are stimulants to the kidneys and heart.

If there's enough poison in one tulip bulb to kill an adult, if sweet • G peas contain enough poison to cause a form of paralysis which, though not fatal, can keep a victim bedridden for several months, and if dieffenbachia can seriously burn the mouth if its stalk is bitten into, then they have no place in homes where inquisitive children reside.

G • The attractive but poisonous berries of the English and American holly, daphne (mezereum), and celastrus are very appealing to young children. Bittersweet is particularly dangerous, as I have found while helping in the local Poison Center for the past few years.

G • Two garden-growing vegetables also present problems: eating or even chewing rhubarb leaves causes painful stomach cramps (due to their content of oxalic acid and compounds); and the potato produces green sprouts (also the shoots, leaves, and stem) which, if consumed, produce mental disorganization and cardiac depression.

G • If you go hunting mushrooms, go only with an expert who can point out to you the deadly amanita and the many other dangerous varieties. (Some experts say not to trust even them. And don't rely on a book; its pictures and descriptions can be inaccurate.)

G • Do you know the difference between the highly toxic water hemlock and Queen Anne's lace? The latter is wild carrot, and its young edible leaves may be cut and put into a soup or stew, or dried and powdered to yield a suitable salt substitute.

ICE CUBES

H • Prepare an extra supply of ice cubes by using plastic egg trays for that purpose. Store the cubes in plastic bags in your freezer.

INSECTS

Be sure to sweep out the dust from under your refrigerator (and • **H**
stove and washer and dryer). Such places are dark, warm, and
damp, and provide excellent breeding grounds for all kinds of
insects and their eggs. Use your vacuum to finish the job. Do this
once a month. A wire coat hanger, bent lengthwise, and with the
loop covered with knotted yarn or cloth, is another great tool for
cleaning under cabinets or appliances.

Avoid hanging strip insecticides in the kitchen or elsewhere in • **H**
your home. The active ingredient of one commercial product
contains a highly toxic compound, dichlorovinyl dimethyl phos-
phate. The label usually contains a caution to this effect: "Do not
get in mouth or eyes; harmful if swallowed. . . . Do not use in
nurseries or rooms where infants or aged persons are confined. Do
not use in kitchens, restaurants, or in areas where food is prepared
or served." A chemical textbook states that this dangerous compound is not permitted in sickrooms.

IRISH MOSS

Grandmother's art of candying flowers (particularly violets and • **G**
rose petals) becomes quite easy when the flowers are gently
dipped into a thin gel of flavored Irish moss and allowed to
become nearly dry. Spread on waxed paper, then sprinkle with
powdered sugar. When thoroughly dry, store in the refrigerator.

The very same Irish moss with which you prepare your highly • **M**
nutritious fruit jelly and various puddings has other, equally
profitable, uses. A big pinch of the moss (or 2 teaspoonfuls of the
plain jelly) simmered in 2 cups of hot pekoe tea and then cooled
and strained, gives a fast soothing lotion for scalds, burns, sunburn, and minor skin irritations. It is available in health food
stores, certain drugstores, and seashore shops.

Or when 2 teaspoonsful of honey and 1 of lemon juice are mixed • **M**
into the plain jelly, this item is not only a good skin lotion but as
good a cough syrup as ever you had.

JERUSALEM ARTICHOKE

F • This food is not native to Jerusalem or the Near East, Jerusalem being a corruption of the Italian word *girasole*, meaning "turning to the sun." Although it does not resemble, and is not, an artichoke, it is related to that green vegetable and has been in constant use since early Greco-Roman times.

The tubers were well known to the American Indians, and Lewis and Clark, for example, were often served "wild" artichokes by Sacajawea. Two centuries earlier, the explorer Champlain observed that the Indians cultivated roots "which taste like an Artichoke." And his contemporary, Lescarbot, so enjoyed the flavorful taste that he took the roots back to France where they were sold under the name of *torpinambaux*. Later, the roots traveled to England, where they were cultivated as "potatoes of Canada," and stewed with dates and raisins.

The Chippewas ate them raw like a radish—we eat ours in salad. The Potawatomi used them as a potatolike foodstuff. The cooked bulbs and the pot liquor were used for kidney troubles by both the Chippewas and the Potawatomi.

F • For optimum food value, the tubers, once well scrubbed in cold water, can be sliced and eaten uncooked, or steamed—but never boiled. Folks do include them in soups, stews, and pea purees —and often pickle the smaller crisp ones or prepare a relish of them. Cook 15 to 20 minutes in hot water, in a covered pot, or steam them 10 minutes or only long enough to soften, and flavor with basil. Only the inner white fleshy part is eaten. They may be chilled and served as a side dish, with favorite dressing. Try marinating a few buds (leaves) before incorporating them in a salad. The jellylike liquid resulting from cooking the roots is a good base for soup.

G • Want a lot of Jerusalem artichokes next year? Buy three or four in a health food store and plant them in loose garden soil, in a sunny location but away from your vegetable garden, because they spread profusely. In the fall of the following year, you'll have a good supply.

During the winter months, we cultivate the tubers indoors, on a • G
plant stand close to the sun-filled windows of our living room, and then steam the leaves.

Jerusalem artichokes are alkaline in reaction, rich in potassium, • M
and also offer large amounts of calcium, sodium, phosphorus, sulfur, iron, chlorine, and magnesium. The protein matter amounts to 2 percent, a wholesome gum 9.1 percent, levulose sugar 4.2 percent, and inulin 1.1 percent. The sugar can be eaten by diabetics; and the starch is represented by inulin, which triples in quantity by fall. Not only have the tubers been used as a specific remedy in pancreatitis and diabetes, but extracts of the plant have been found effective against the staphylococcus and Escherichia bacteria.

JUNIPER

Juniper berries are used to flavor gin and to prepare vinegars and • F
marinating mixtures When used to flavor soup, stew, or sauce, they should be tied in cheesecloth or cloth bag and removed at serving time.

Juniper shrubs grow wild in clayey or rocky areas and on dry hills; • G
their ripe fruits are available in October.

Taken with demulcent and aromatic herbs, Juniper berries are of • M
special benefit in simple kidney disorders and for mild indigestion. They have served well as a stimulating diuretic in cystitic and catarrhal conditions of the urinary system.

We have used the dried ripe fruits for other purposes also. To • H
disinfect or cleanse a room of foul odors, put a teaspoonful of them in a pan of hot water and the rising vapors will diffuse throughout the room. Or place the pan of hot water and the berries on a warm radiator or stove. Interesting that for centuries juniper and rosemary were used in French hospitals as disinfectants.

57

KITCHEN ACCESSORIES

CORN MILL, COFFEE GRINDER

F • These instruments coarsely grind or finely powder a variety of seeds and grains, herbs and spices, and the leaves of vegetables and "weeds."
Mill these foods: sunflower and sesame seeds, wheat, rye, oats, barley, corn, rice, millet, and buckwheat.

JUICERS

F • Indispensable to dieters and those on a detoxifying program. This is an excellent way to eat vegetables in liquid form without the bulk or cellulose—occasionally or only 1 or 2 days a week. A juicer must be rustproof and 100 percent stainless steel wherever the fresh juices touch the appliance, from blade and basket to the juice receptacle and pouring spout. Friends find that with fresh vegetable juices available, soda pop, ice cream, canned juices, and nutritionless commercial drinks are a thing of the past.

BLENDER

Incorporate various food items to prepare creams, spreads, dress- • **F**
ings, and so on. The blended vegetable permits one to eat the
entire food—the juice plus the cellulose.

SPROUTER

Produces sprouted seeds, certain beans, and grains that yield a • **F**
concentrated and more nutritious food than when full grown.
Examples: mung and soybeans, lentils, wheat, barley, oats, rye,
and grass seeds.

YOGURT MAKER

Yogurt is a nutritious food that is prepared easily and at very low • **F**
cost. It may be substituted for soured cream, mixed with cottage
cheese, and/or mixed with salad vegetables. It blends smoothly in
salad dressings and creamy sauces.

STEAMER:

Live steam quickly softens the fibers of foods that cannot be • **F**
digested raw. Examples: parsnips, turnips, squash. Such heat
helps to retain the valuable nutrients and the garden-fresh taste.
This utensil is invaluable when making friends with the wild
growing, edible herbs ("weeds").

KITCHEN GARDEN

When I was growing up, a familiar and pleasant place was • **F**
our kitchen garden, conveniently situated a few steps from the
back door. Its approximate 10-by-40 foot dimensions spread the
width of our house. This gardening space was given plenty of
tender, loving care: its plentiful yield of assorted vegetables,
herbs, and flowers testified to that.

To have a kitchen garden today, one need not live in the
country. A space 5 by 20 feet will suffice, providing the soil has
been organically readied and at least 7 to 9 hours of full sunshine

are available. Plan at the end of summer which vegetables and seasoning herbs you will want to plant the following spring, where they will be planted, and especially where you'll prepare small compost piles. September is a good time to turn the soil and begin to add a thin layer of dried manure. Composting one's vegetable refuse in the nearby garden is both convenient and practical. To the refuse one should add grass, fallen leaves, coarsely ground twig cuttings, mucky soil found along brooks, sawdust, weeded-out material, and a layer of soil (even gravelly sand) to each layer of refuse. Once a week stir well and turn these piles over to present a uniform mixture. Space the piles about 15 feet apart. During late fall and winter when composting is not possible, place the refuse over the turned soil intended only for vegetable gardening, and not where your small herb patch is to be.

Aromatic herbs require poor but well-drained soil. If cultivated in good or enriched soil, the foliage may be profuse, but the concentration of aromatic oils will be small. Devote three-quarters of garden space to cultivating the vegetables and the balance to the seasoning herbs.

In spring, as soon as the soil is soft and can be turned over, seeds of the "easy growers" are planted—carrots, beets, turnips, and radishes. When the seedlings are three to four inches high, hoe the rows and reseed. Their mature roots are best eaten raw, in a salad, but by all means do include the greens in your diet.

Early spring also calls for planting dwarf peas which need no stakes, onions, parsnips, and lettuce (but the half-hardy leeks and endive wait for warmer weather). Plant pole and lima beans in late spring since they may be hurt by continued cool weather.

The success of a small kitchen garden depends on:

Continuous plantings. Plant beets or parsley (even cabbage) in a space from which an early crop like peas has been taken: then kale or turnip after green beans, and so on.

Planting the seeds properly. Cover with enough soil to measure three to four times the seed's diameter; in cool weather and thicker soil, a little less; and in warmer weather and lighter loose soil, a little more.

Use the thoroughly mixed composted material as a mulch to your growing (4- to 6-inch) plants. After either a rain soaking of several hours or prolonged watering, place flat stones upon that material as a further mulch. And that's all the watering necessary the *whole* summer.

An easily prepared liquid fertilizer will produce spectacularly increased healthy crops. This is especially necessary if the soil is poor or newly turned over. Stir 1 teaspoonful of dried horse or cow manure well in a wide-mouthed gallon container of water (rain water preferred) and let stand several days in the sunshine or a warm area. Pour about 1 tablespoonful of the strained liquid into a gallon jar of water, add 1 or 2 handfuls of nearby herbs, dried and cut, and let this bask another 2 or 3 days.

KITCHEN HERB GARDEN

The herb section requires about 5 square feet of garden space, divided evenly for annuals and perennials. Of the former, dill, basil, chervil, and summer savory; of the latter, oregano, thyme, burnet, sage, lemon balm, rosemary, among others. Be careful not to apply fertilizers, to overwater, or to add mulching material. You may take 2 or 3 leaf cuttings—from the upper third—of the full-grown herbs just before flowering. Seeds are gathered before they fully ripen. All herb parts should be dried in a room with good circulation, either by suspension—tied in bunches—or on trays, which must be shaken daily. Be sure to label each collection with the name of herb and date gathered.

If your gardening space is rather limited, improvise a "roof garden" of wooden boxes or an herb "wheel." Transplant a few

• **F**

wild-growing mints to an overwet area or next to your garage or house foundation. Beg or borrow a few catnip seeds and plant a few in the vegetable patch, there to grow and not be transplanted.

Border the herb and vegetable sections with chervil, parsley, thyme, chives or wild garlic, marigold, sweet marjoram, and nasturtiums. You'll be pleased with their beauty as well as their usefulness. Moreover, aromatic herbs offer some noteworthy uses: They serve as companion plants to vegetables if grown in their vicinity and greatly aid in repelling the activity of vegetable-harming bugs, aphids, and soil nematodes. For example, nasturtiums go with radishes, broccoli, and squash; marigolds with rosebushes, tomatoes, and potatoes; chamomile with wheat (ratio is 1 to 100), onions (one plant every 12 feet), and cabbage; summer savory with beans; rosemary with carrots; and chervil with and eaten with radishes. Such companionship often indicates which foods go best with which herbs: tomatoes by basil, beans by summer savory, cabbage by chamomile, and so on.

Equally important for the kitchen gardener to remember: When you weed the vegetable or herb patch, take care *not* to discard those weedy nondescripts just because *you* don't know their names and aren't aware of their kitchen uses and health-saving values. Chivelike wild garlic, pussley (purslane), evening primrose, early dandelion and yellow dock, amaranth (pigweed), and goosefoot (lamb's-quarters) make good salad greens and ingredients for soup, stew, and casserole, and the fruits (seeds) of the latter three herbs we have used in herb cookies and leavened bread. Furthermore, most herbs, when dried and coarsely cut, become admirable remedies for a variety of ailments: dandelion, pussley, ground ivy (gill-over-the-ground), and witchgrass for kidney problems; dandelion, yellow dock, and evening primrose for liver, stomach, and bloodstream. Violets, wild garlic, and primrose serve in bronchial disorders. (Perhaps you didn't realize that most fruits and vegetables possess medicinal properties.)

KNIVES

H • Those cardboard rolls found in wax paper or foil make individual holders for long, sharp knives. Flatten the roll and close one end with staples or heavy thread. The knives are better protected —and so are you—and they're safely stored in a drawer.

Tips to keep knives in good condition: Always cut foods on a wooden board to protect the knife's edge and your tablecloth or countertop. Wash knives separately. • **H**

Have knives sharpened periodically. You won't have to bear down so hard to make them cut, and there's less chance of their slipping. A dull knife can be a dangerous implement. • **H**

Don't substitute knives for screwdriver, scissors, or bottle opener. Use them for the chores for which they were meant. • **H**

LECITHIN

I advocate eating whole, unprocessed foods, not partial ones such as lecithin, protein powders, and desiccated liver. Nor do I recommend vitamin/mineral supplements, tablets of bee pollen, whey, "vegetable salad," which in recent years have joined the "health food" cures. Lecithin has become a popular food because of its purported antigallstone and anticholesterol action, and since it is mistakenly thought to be a food-medicine, it is consumed in many ways—with scrambled eggs, baked goods, gravy, and sauce, foods that should be avoided. But since soybeans are an excellent source, then that lecithin-containing food is the item to eat. Sprout them for optimum nutritives. • **F**

LEFTOVERS

Don't throw away the last few particles that won't leave the bottom of the catsup and chili sauce bottles. Just add a little hot water to the bottle, shake well, and season a gravy or meat with the remaining liquid. • **F**

Create a novel soup specialty by first blending any vegetable odds and ends, such as celery bottoms and leaves, parsley stems, chicory leaves, and other cooked leftovers. (See SOUP.) • **F**

F • Chop leftover lima beans and mix with peas, corn, fresh carrot, and radish. Add a little French or Russian dressing or sour cream, and season with herbs. A delicious side dish that goes well with fish.

F • Recently refrigerated or frozen egg whites can be added to cake recipes. Stale bread becomes melba toast, soup croutons, or bread crumbs. Baked or boiled potatoes and vegetables can be added to a casserole or cooked in a soup or stew. Leftover meats or poultry—sliced, diced, minced, chopped, or ground—can be baked into pies or patties or croquettes. Soups or consommé may be used in stews, casseroles, hash, shepherd's pie, gravy, or marinating liquids. (See COFFEE.)

H • Save frozen potpie foil pans and use them to store cold leftover foods. Cover the pans with the plastic tops from 2-pound coffee cans, which fit them nicely. Thus the pans are made stackable and save refrigerator space. And you'll save time and trouble for, with the lid removed, the food can be reheated in the pans.

LEMON

F • Lemon juice and ground lemon peel help to tenderize chicken. Before cooking, rub the juice onto inside and outside and disperse the peels throughout the cavity.

F • If only a little juice is needed, don't cut the fruit. Pierce with a skewer, squeeze out the required amount, and replace in the refrigerator.

F • If it's more juice you want, soak the lemon in cold water before squeezing. Placing in hot water or in a heated oven may produce more juice, but the juice is inferior in taste and nutrients.

F • The juice and finely grated peel do wonders for berry pies.

F • Save the rinds, after using the juice. Fresh, they can be grated into salads, slaw, chicken or turkey stuffings, casseroles, and so on. Dried, they may be used to flavor tea, and finely ground or grated, to season mayonnaise, salad dressings, soups and stews, cakes, pastry, and breads. Refrigerate dried whole rinds. Grind or grate them only when needed.

Try planting lemon seeds in well-drained soil. These house plants • G make pretty little shrubs. The leaves fresh or dried may be used whole to flavor applesauce and fruit compotes, stews, salads, carrots. Or the leaves may be ground and used as the rind is.

Chilled? Sore throat? Getting a cold? Try a warm drink of lemon • M juice and warm water sweetened with honey every two or three hours.

Lemon juice will remove food stains from men's ties (silk). Add a • H little lemon juice to a regular spot remover. This method will keep the tie from fading. (First, test the liquid on the back of the tie.)

An uncovered peel will absorb refrigerator odors and add its own • H fresh smell to that area.

Lemon juice is a must in European beauty salons. Not only is it • C incorporated in facial and skin applications, it is an often-used rinse following shampoos and particularly valuable for dandruff treatments, by being vigorously massaged into the scalp before shampooing.

LINIMENTS

A quick-acting rubefacient liniment and counterirritant, which • M warms the affected area and so helps to relieve pain, may easily be prepared with kitchen ingredients. Dissolve ½ ounce of crushed camphor in an ounce of rubbing alcohol. Add this solution and 2 teaspoonsful of weak ammonia water to 3 ounces of olive oil. Shake well and apply gently. Do not bandage.

Another liniment useful for those post-exercise or jogging charley • M horses is easily made in your kitchen laboratory. Mix 4 ounces each of olive oil (or other vegetable oil) and of turpentine. In this dissolve 2 teaspoonsful of coarsely cut camphor. Add 4 ounces of any herb vinegar. If a warmer embrocation is desired and time is available, steep a tablespoonful of ground red pepper in this mixture (previously warmed slightly) for 1 or 2 hours, stir, and strain. Allow to cool and add the other ingredients. Finally, combine 1 ounce of wintergreen oil and enough witch hazel to make 1 pint. Shake well before using.

LINOLEUM

H • When washing your linoleum, add ¼ cup of vinegar to a quart of light soapsuds. This acts as a cleanser and color brightener and gives a nice polish.

MARGARINE

F • Margarine is a nonnatural, synthetic, and harmful food. The danger arises from its saturated and hydrogenated fats. The only reason that vegetable oils are hydrogenated (hydrogen saturated) is to prepare commercially a smooth, soft solid which will satisfy taste and economy. The consumer has been also attracted to this health-destroyer by its pleasant odor, nice taste, and long life. Certainly this most unreasonable facsimile of butter must be recognized as a harmful and far less nutritious product, since too few of its constituents are natural and wholesome. Nonhydrogenated margarines are found in health food stores.

The addition of yellow coloring matter presents a further health problem: Yellow No. 3 (AB) and No. 4 (OB) which are found in edible fats, margarine, butter, cakes, biscuits, and candies are unsafe in ordinary amounts, and must be considered potentially dangerous additives to foods.

Certain margarines are not as "vegetable" as they appear to be: some still contain lard and fats from fish or whales, glycerides, isopropyl, citrated, monoisopropyl citrate (a stabilizer), emulsifiers, salt, excess water, pasteurized skimmed milk, artificial flavoring, synthetic vitamins A and D, and preservatives.
Some of the oils may be very close to the point of putrefaction before they are processed, while many of the vegetable oils are

66

rendered by a harsh caustic solvent (such as hexane gas, a highly toxic chemical solvent). Refining of the oil undergoes several chemical treatments under very high temperatures.

Hydrogenation of any living substance or organism is fatal to them; moreover, the process takes place only in the presence of chemical catalysts such as finely powdered nickel, platinum, cobalt, or paladium, *which can never be completely removed from the oil.* (See BUTTER)

MARIGOLDS

Cultivate marigolds in the kitchen garden, not only for their decorative value, but even more for their seasoning and tinting effects. Dried, they may be used with rice, potato, and pastries as an inexpensive substitute for the expensive saffron flowers. Save your marigold flower heads when fully expanded and dry them. Powder or grind the flowers only as needed.

• F

A French herbalist's liver and gall bladder remedy: Steep 3 or 4 teaspoonsful of dried marigold flowers in a cupful (8 ounces) of *cold* water overnight. Add this and 2 heaping teaspoonsful of ground dried orange peels to 3 cups of hot water and boil, *covered,* down to half the liquid amount. When cool, stir and strain. Add enough honey to sweeten. The dose is 2 teaspoonsful in a little water 3 times a day and upon retiring.

• M

You can prepare an effective healing lotion merely by covering any amount of marigold heads with rubbing alcohol (not iso-propyl) and letting it sit for 4 to 5 days at room temperature. Stir daily and strain after the 4th or 5th day. Dilute with an equal amount of water. Apply to scratches and cuts. At one time, I prepared a similar (undiluted) remedy for dentists for use in infections and ulcers of mouth and gums.

• M

Herbalists have long employed marigolds for feverish colds, eyewashes, children's inflammatory diseases, and "aches and pains."

• M

One may use marigolds for skin problems by steeping 2 tea-spoonsful of petals in 2 ounces of alcohol for 10 to 15 days. Or slowly simmer for 10 minutes a level tablespoon of petals in 3 to 4

• C

ounces of melted, unsalted lard. Both products must be strained, and the latter should be refrigerated. They're suitable as healing agents for simple cuts and irritated sores. In my pharmacy I've prepared a skin cleansing (astringent) lotion by covering any amount of flower heads with witch hazel, letting it steep for a week or two, and straining.

C • Blondes will find an infusion of marigolds a lovely hair lightener by using it as an after-shampoo rinse.

MARINATING

F • A marinade softens coarse meats, game, or fish, and helps reduce the amount of dangerous fat from such foods. Meats are also flavored as well as tenderized. In many cases, stomach disorders are prevented since obnoxious toxins in the meat are well counteracted by this process.

F • If you have had problems seasoning turkey or chicken, try using a marinade, which will invariably flavor either bird far better than any stuffing. A marinade becomes a basting fluid when so needed, as well as a preseasoned gravy or sauce. The remaining solution may be saved and rewarmed when needed to serve as a sauce for other meats.

F • Indeed, the chefs of many high-priced restaurants practice the marinating of foods for some 8 to 10 hours, at a low heat, turning over and basting the food once an hour or so for uniform marinating.

F • As a rule, herb-marinated foods need no further flavoring when served—no salt, no pickles, no relish. And yes, excellent digestion. The ingredients of herb marinades are as follows:
The liquids: lemon juice, vermouth, or other white wine (unless otherwise specified), safflower or corn oil, cider vinegar, herb vinegar of your choice, and chicken stock.
The seasoners: basil; caraway; chervil; chives; dill (seed or whole herb); fennel; garlic; juniper berries; the dried rinds of lemon, lime, orange, and tangerine; oregano; parsley; rosemary; sage; savory; tarragon; and thyme.

Also used are wild grape and cabbage leaves, good to tenderize deer, hare, pheasant, or quail.

MARJORAM

Did you know that marjoram is good in almost everything you cook? In stuffings, salads, cheese dishes and their dressings, meats, fish, and cooked vegetables.

• **F**

A half teaspoon of marjoram and ¼ teaspoon of oregano steeped 10 minutes in hot water soothe a nervous or disordered stomach. The strained liquid may be taken every 1 or 2 hours.

• **M**

MAYONNAISE

Do try to do with a minimum of store-bought mayonnaise, which is artificial and nutritionless.
When foods are properly seasoned i.e., with culinary herbs—store-bought mayonnaise is hardly needed.

• **F**

Prepare your own:
    ½ cup herb or cider vinegar
    1 egg
    1 teaspoon honey
    ½ teaspoon sea salt (optional)
    1½ cups vegetable oil
Blend the first four ingredients well. Then add the oil slowly and continue to blend until the mixture is uniform and thick. Place in a covered bottle or jar and let stay at room temperature for an hour or so. Then refrigerate until needed.

• **F**

With a little skill, you too can vary the herb seasonings to make a mayonnaise to suit your taste. Vary the taste of your mayonnaise with greens and herbs: parsley, chives, chervil, carrot tops, basil, dill, tarragon, oregano, and others you like. For example:
    2 cups mayonnaise
    2 tablespoons minced parsley
    1 tablespoon minced chives
    ½ tablespoon dill herb
    Blend well.

• **F**

Using mayonnaise? Add ¼ cup of diced celery and 1 tablespoon of chives, and if available, ½ teaspoonful of minced fresh dill to a cupful of the spread. When making a dip, add a tablespoon of crumbled cheese, stir in the juice of a clove of garlic, cover tightly, and refrigerate a few hours to blend the flavors. Add ¼ to ½ teaspoon of curry powder or a squirt of lemon or lime juice to give extra zest.

Why not prepare several smaller-sized jars of differently flavored spreads?

H • A mayonnaise stain should be first soaked in cold water, then washed in warm soapy water and rinsed thoroughly. Allow to dry. If the stain persists, apply a grease solvent like naphtha. (Do the same for a meat stain.)

C • Your homemade mayonnaise (containing vegetable oil) is a good cleanser and quickly penetrating agent for sensitive skin, especially after overexposure to cold, wind, or sun. The major ingredient of the spread—the vegetable oil—penetrates the skin more deeply than the mineral oils usually found in skin creams. The egg yolk provides a grand source of vitamin A, essential for correct skin nourishment. And the (cider) vinegar supplies the acidity necessary to maintain proper pH (alkaline-acid) balance.

MEAT SUBSTITUTES

F • Meat substitutes are the thing with rocketing meat prices. Surprising how easy it is to reach a high protein level on a meatless diet. Everything that grows in nature offers appreciable amounts of protein (amino acids). Obviously, the grains upon which animals feed should be included in our diet. One needs to consider the total intake of daily protein and the variety of amino acids found in each food.

Navy, lima, soya, mung, and adsuki beans contain substantia. amounts of amino acids, enzymes, minerals, starch, and sugar. Soak in water at least 10 to 12 hours before cooking. Season with aromatic herbs of your choice—savory, basil, dill, or sage.
Eat more cheese. Parmesan has 35 percent protein content, better

than meat (20 to 30 percent), closely followed by nuts, peas, seeds, and lentils (20 to 25 percent). Eggs and milk, as concentrated foods, contain far less protein.

Use cottage cheese as a spread instead of margarine or butter. Peanut butter? Many food stores prepare it fresh. I've never made any peanut butter myself, but friends who have suggest using a Moulinex-type coffee or spice grinder. They use small amounts of unroasted peanuts (with or without cashews). The result is a chunky, not fine, peanut butter. A smooth type is created with the addition of a vegetable oil like sesame or sunflower. Delicious on a celery stick.

Bake your own bread with basic seed-flour: millet, rye, wheat, and sesame. These must be undegerminated and organically raised. (Soya flour yields over 40 percent protein.)

You can overcome the high cost of meats and fish by eating more dairy foods, nuts, grains, and legumes. The following is an abbreviated chart showing the protein content of foods, based on 100 grams of edible portions:

Meats

Beef: chuck, cooked 18.0 =	26.0 grams
porterhouse, cooked	23.0
liver, cooked	26.6
Chicken: broiled	20.2
Ham: broiled	22.8
Lamb and mutton	16.0
Lamb: chop	24.0
Pork	12.0
Turkey	20.1
Veal: cooked	28.0

Fish

Flounder: raw	14.9
Haddock: cooked or fried	18.7
Herring: smoked or kippered	22.2
Mackerel: raw (average)	20.0
Salmon: baked or broiled	28.0

Dairy

Cheddar	25.0
Cottage	19.5
Egg yolk	16.3

*Legumes
and nuts*

Beans	22.1
Cashews: roasted or cooked	18.5
Chickpeas:	20.8
Fava	23.4
Lentil: whole	24.0
Lima	19.7
Mung	23.9
Peas: entire seeds 22.5	-23.8
Peanuts: roasted and shelled	26.9
Soya beans: whole, dried 35	-38

COMPARATIVE RATINGS OF PROTEINS, GIVING PERCENTAGE OF USABLE PROTEIN

Soya powder (low fat)	38.0
Wheat germ	22.9
Peanuts	15.0
Whole egg	12.0
Oatmeal (rolled)	13.0
Whole wheat	12.2
Lima beans	8.2
Rye (whole)	11.0
Rice, brown	7.5
Corn, whole	5.5
Cow's milk (whole)	3.5
Potatoes	2.0

MELONS

F • Melons should be eaten alone, chewed well, and not accompanied by other foods. They are most suitable during the summer months since they contain both highly mineralized food and drink, "a drink," states Dr. William Esser, "more pure than that of a mountain stream." Alone, melons cause no distress, but if eaten as the meal's appetizer or as dessert, or taken with ice cream, stomach distress may occur. The starch and sugar of ice cream and melon interrupt the digestion of previous courses— especially concentrated flour products (bread, cereals, sugars) and proteins (meats, egg, dairy products). As a result, destructive fermentation of the carbohydrates and putrefaction of the proteins occurs, creating an overacid condition. This food is alkaline, a "water food," offers good amounts of vitamins A, B_1, C, and blood-fortifying minerals of calcium, sodium, magnesium, phosphorus, and potassium.

Eat melons at room temperature for their best taste. (See FRUIT.)

MINERAL OIL

There are serious objections to using mineral oil. Taken as a laxative, it leaches out vitamins A, D, E, and K from the blood and tissues. Perhaps that was the reason that, as early as 1937, great fear was expressed that it possessed the carcinogenic effects of crude oil. It is also said to inhibit the absorption of bile from the intestines, thereby preventing pancreatic digestion. • M

Externally, say the nutritionists, mineral oil (or baby oil, for example), penetrates the skin and may again deplete the blood of the above named vitamins. Nursing mothers should therefore not apply baby oil to their nipples. • M

Baby oil is at best a mild skin lubricant, a superficial emollient, and a fair makeup remover. As it appears on drug shelves, it consists mostly of mineral oil. The oil works better when mixed with an equal part of safflower or other light-colored vegetable oil. • C

MILK

Milk is not the food it is supposed to be, regardless of the high-pressure advertising. The pasteurization process destroys • F

73

almost entirely the vitamins, especially A, B, and C, and enzymes so necessary to ensure complete digestion of the milk solids. Raw milk is far preferable to pasteurized and dried skim milk contains ten times more calcium, phosphorus, and iron than pasteurized. Once tampered with, milk becomes a deceptive food and not the "must" food that is mistakenly taken for granted. If you must have dairy products, then have goat's milk, soured cream, clabber, yogurt, and cottage or farmer's cheese.

A warm drink before retiring: Put ½ teaspoonful of ground sage leaves in warm milk, cover, and simmer gently 2 to 3 minutes. Cover until cool enough to drink.—Mrs. T.J.H., a former student of my herb class.

M • An old remedy: Milk may be applied as a wet compress for the temporary relief of acute sores, eczema, etc.

F • Drink no milk (or water or other liquids) with your meal. Drink it alone or leave it alone.

M • Quick remedy for diarrhea: To a cupful of hot milk add two large pinches of powdered cinnamon and one of powdered cloves.

M • Grandfather's remedy for an irritating cough: Mix a teaspoonful of honey and sesame or other vegetable oil in a cup of warm milk and sip it slowly.

M • Suffer an eye burn or accidental irritation due to table salt or spice? Insert 1 or 2 drops of milk in each corner of the eye.

H • Milk stains must first be sponged well with cool water. Then rub in a detergent, let remain awhile, and rinse the area thoroughly.

MINT

F • Mint is much used to season peas, potatoes, and other starchy foods. When you're making herb vinegar or jelly, use your own garden mint and you'll enjoy them more. Flavor a sauce intended for chicken or lamb with spearmint or orangemint for a new taste delight.

F • A "northern" julep may be prepared by steeping ½ teaspoonful each of mint, catnip, and basil, ¼ teaspoonful each of sage, and dried orange or lemon peel. A ritual among Near Eastern peoples is the drinking of "Turkish tea," which consists of an infusion of spearmint and lemon or orange peel.

I consider mint one of those indispensable kitchen herbs. It is • **G**
indeed a most "friendly herb." Once you've located it growing on
the banks of a nearby brook, transplant the roots and a ball of the
soil into your garden and also into a wide-mouthed flowerpot
filled with mucky or rich soil and small stones. Be sure to water it
often. Good for kitchen (windowsill) garden.

MUSHROOMS

Mushrooms are the "in" food and quite popular these days in • **F**
kitchen and restaurant. The appetite for them appears to be
insatiable, and they're now sold commercially—fresh, canned,
frozen, and dried. Picking mushrooms is dangerous! Public
health officials warn self-styled "experts" that there is always
danger of killing themselves. Without adequate testing means, it
is sometimes impossible to tell which species are poisonous.
Beware of trying to recognize the safe species; the differences are
slight enough to result in fatal errors. Avoid picking any after a
rain. Boiling them with silver coins or spoons is quite useless.
Mushrooms are easily grown in your cellar. Takes only a small
space and the investment is low.

How nutritive are mushrooms? Their mineral content—calcium, • **F**
iron, and potassium—is most inconsequential, as is their protein
value. Their nutritional claim rests on a good amount of niacin
(4.8 mg per cup) and riboflavin (B_2), and thiamin (B_1) in small
amounts. They key to the food's appeal lies in its high proportion
of glutamic acid. However, any food that grows without air,
water, and in darkness (without the sun's benefit) is not fit for
man or animal. The longer they're cooked, the more rubbery and
indigestible they become and tend to decay in the stomach rather
than being absorbed and assimilated.

F • Mushrooms (although their food value is nil) may be sliced thin and incorporated into a vegetable salad. They may also be marinated and served as a side dish. Slice the tops and stems of a pound of large mushrooms and place them in a bowl with 1 small white onion, 2 tablespoons chives or 1 tablespoon of garlic greens or shallot greens, all minced. The marinade: ¼ cup basil or tarragon vinegar, ¼ cup white wine, ⅔ cup sesame or peanut oil, garlic clove, 1½ tablespoons ground lemon rind. Mix the ingredients well and let the mushrooms soak in the mixture for an hour. Stir every 10 minutes or so. Before serving, sprinkle them with chopped parsley.

MUSTARD

F • Powdered or prepared mustard should not be used as food seasoning. Its strong volatile oil is too irritating to the delicate mucous lining of the stomach and intestines. It is probably on your doctor's list of forbidden foods.

M • For a recent painful bruise or swelling, make a thick poultice of the powder with hot water and apply it, wrapping a linen or similar cloth around it, for 10 to 15 minutes.

M • To make a jiffy, pain-relieving salve, mix 1 teaspoonful of powdered mustard and ½ teaspoonful of powdered ginger or red pepper with an ounce of chicken fat, goose grease, or mutton suet.

H • To remove odors from smelly bottles, pour a little hot water with a generous pinch of mustard powder into each bottle. Shake and let stand overnight. Then rinse with hot water.

n

NASTURTIUMS

F • Add extra zest to your vegetable salad with a few early leaves and the red-orange flowers of nasturtiums that adorn your windows or flower garden. This addition has long been enjoyed as a delicacy

by many Asian peoples. And around the early 1800s, the plants • **F**
were commonly grown in English vegetable gardens along with
carrots, peas, and other vegetables. The nutritional value is
similar to that of watercress.

Including nasturtiums in our salads will teach us to partake more • **F**
of such native (weedy) edibles as watercress (a close relative),
dandelion, peppergrass, sorrel, and wild onion.

The flower buds and half-ripened seeds may be pickled to
produce "French capers." These parts, and the older leaves and
stems, when steeped a few days in a jar containing pickle juice,
may be added to warm and cold dishes.

If you're going to cultivate nasturtiums in porch boxes, window • **G**
gardens, or hanging baskets, use fairly rich soil.

NECTARINE

The nectarine is a fuzzless peach and has been known for thou- • **F**
sands of years. It is now in commercial cultivation on the West
Coast. Since nectarines appear on nectarine trees and sometimes
on peach trees, one may presume that the food values of these two
foods are about the same. A cup of the sliced fruits has as much
protein matter as 10 green olives and is rich in vitamin A, iron,
calcium, and nicotinic acid.

Nectarines are delicious with apricots, apples, grapes, papaya, • **F**
blackberries, raspberries, and cherries.

NERVES

A simple remedy for nervous headache: Mix equal parts of • **M**
ground mint, catnip, sage, chamomile, and marjoram, and steep
a teaspoonful of this mixture in a cup of hot water. Sprinkle about
½ to ¾ teaspoonful celery seeds over the liquid. Cover and let
stand 15 to 20 minutes. Stir and strain. Sip slowly; better take a
teaspoonful at a time. Drink 1 cupful every 2 to 3 hours if
necessary.

At the slightest sign of a headache, nervous upset, or indigestion, • **M**
stop eating. Skip the next meal or two and lie down.

NUTMEG

F • Nutmeg is a rather large seed that is sold as is or ground and sold in ½-ounce containers.

F • Nutmeg has many culinary uses: in rice pudding, many desserts, eggnog, egg dishes, cheese dishes. I know of two cooks who use nutmeg in meat and in mashed and baked potatoes. It is used either alone or with allspice, ginger, or cinnamon, or in spice blend formulas for mincemeat, poultry, and sausage. In my herbal practice, I found folks using it in fancy condiments such as catsup and chutney, to spice up applesauce, apple pie, and baked apples and in diverse sauces, puddings, and jellies. Restaurant chefs use the ground nut to flavor cooked starchy vegetables like cauliflower, potato, and cabbage, and in "exotic recipes" for scrambled eggs and split pea soup. One seed should go a long way in your flavoring endeavor.

G • A friend who greatly enjoys the taste of nutmeg added a nutmeg geranium to his window garden so that he could use the dried leaves in his herb teas.

H • In large doses nutmeg is narcotic, but in small doses the spice is helpful for curing nervous stomach conditions and resulting headaches. Nutmeg has also traditionally been used to prevent insomnia. For this purpose, crush half a nutmeg and steep it in hot water.

NUTS

F • Nuts are an excellent source of unsaturated fats, minerals, vitamins (especially A and B-complex factors), and proteins. This admirable staple food should be taken as *meat*, as one's protein, and not wasted as party fare or as a dessert.

F • Nuts are best eaten *unroasted* and taken with salad vegetables or acid fruits (grapefruit or orange). Roasting enhances the flavor and color of nuts, but has an adverse reaction on liver and gallbladder.

F • Shelled nuts must be tightly covered and refrigerated.

One hundred grams of the edible portion of the following nuts present these protein values (compared to chicken—18.0): almond, 18.6 grams; Brazil, 14.4; cashew, 18.5; pecans, 9.4; and walnut, 15.0.

• F

Vegetarians find nuts, beans, and sprouted seeds an excellent source of unsaturated fats, minerals, proteins, and other nutrients. They're far more nutritious than excessively high-priced meats which are often heavily laden with the dangerous cholesterol-bearing fat and uric acid compounds.

• F

A variety of nut trees exists throughout the United States and abound especially in New England. (Members of my herb-study class prepare bread with acorns.)

• G

This demulcent remedy cleanses and soothes acne, pimples, and similar skin eruptions. Pound several almonds and an equal portion of rice to a meal and rub into the skin. If the skin is overdry, blend in a little vegetable oil.

• C

A good skin cleanser is easily prepared by mixing 1 teaspoonful of borax, 2 of kaolin (obtainable at the drugstore), and 2 ounces of almond meal. This powder serves well to cleanse inflamed skin.

• C

OATMEAL

Here's a first-rate facial: soak overnight 1 tablespoon of rolled (quick cooking) oats in 2 tablespoons of buttermilk and incorporate one beaten egg white. Spread over the face and neck and let it stay 20 to 30 minutes. Remove with a washcloth and unheated water. Do this twice a day.

• C

Use an oatmeal facial to cleanse oily skin. Apply a thin paste of ground and cooked oatmeal strained into whole milk, to the face, let it rest a few minutes, and remove with tepid water. (A commercially prepared product containing oatmeal is said to make the bath soothing and to leave the skin velvety soft.)

• C

C • Mix enough honey into (uncooked) oatmeal to soften it sufficiently to spread on the face. (If too thick, add a little water.) Let stay there 20 to 30 minutes and wash it off with tepid water.

C • Leftover breakfast (prepared) oatmeal mixed with equal parts of bay rum or witch hazel is a great face lotion.

For oatmeal as a food, see GRAINS.

ODDS AND ENDS

H • A handy gadget: Save the tiny metal clip that dry cleaners use to hold skirts on hangers. They have other uses: they fasten full wastebasket liners when ready for the trash, clip together notes and papers, coupons, recipes, memos, and grocery lists. They may also be used as markers for your sewing or knitting.

H • Those wire twists that keep bread packages closed are most serviceable as repair agents for torn, loose, or broken wicker furniture. Either weave them into the wicker or glue them around the legs and other supports. After the furniture has been so repaired, paint the twists to blend in.

ODORS

H • A kitchen filled with undesirable cooking odors can be quickly refreshed. Place a little cinnamon and a clove bud, or ½ teaspoonful each of dried mint, rosemary, eucalyptus, or other pleasantly aromatic herbs in a pint of hot water. Place over a warm oven or radiator. Their resultant moist, sweet-smelling aromas effectively counteract offensive odors.

H • Also: Set ¼ cup of herb vinegar on the stove next to frying foods. Especially good for a poorly ventilated kitchen.

H • How to create welcome odors:
Roast pounded coffee on an iron plate.
Burn sugar on hot coals.
Boil vinegar with myrrh (available from your druggist).

Refrigerator: • **H**
Keep a few drops of oil of wintergreen or a piece of charcoal in an open box in a rear corner.

You may also make a wash of hot water and a little powdered mustard to remove lingering odors. (This wash is also good to remove stubborn odors from jars and bottles. Let stand for a few hours before again rinsing in hot water.)

An aromatic vinegar helps the atmosphere of a smoke-laden • **H** room. One friend puts small bowls of it in the four corners of her living room when smokers congregate. Another friend uses a small dish of activated charcoal to remove postparty odors.

To remove the odors of plastic containers, soak them with baking • **H** soda and water (2 teaspoonsful to a quart) for several hours. Another "worked well for me" method is to fill the container with water, cover, and place in the freezer. Remove when frozen, place the bottom in warm water, and with the removal of the ice the odor goes.

I know of a chef who removes the odor of onion from his chopping • **H** knife and his hands by simply rubbing both with a slice of fresh tomato—not canned. He claims the odor disappears like magic.

And a tomato juice and vinegar wash will remove most of the • **H** skunk smell from a sprayed dog.

Coffee grounds kept in an open container help eliminate the • **H** mustiness of closets, cellars, and even the refrigerator. (The grounds also serve the gardener by ensuring an acid condition of the soil where needed.)

A small camphor cake serves your kitchen garbage pail as a • **H** deodorizer and antiseptic.

OIL

Which vegetable oil is best? Certainly one must first eliminate all • **F** commercial trade brands. Their actual oil content by percentages is rarely revealed on the label. Recommended oils are unprocessed safflower, corn germ, peanut, sesame, and soya bean.

F • When refrigerating oil-based salad dressings and marinated foods, use safflower and corn oils. They don't solidify when refrigerated, even over a prolonged period. But for all general purposes—baking, frying, cooking, or using with herbs—all unprocessed oils are acceptable. (Unless olive oil is "virgin . . . first press," use only as a last resort.) Be sure that the label states that no additives or chemical preservatives have been added, that the oil has not been refined or bleached, and is free from solvents and dyes.

F • These oils have a high ratio of polyunsaturated to saturated fats (safflower—9 to 1, corn—2 to 1), are rich in vitamin E and natural lecithin, and are therefore good for all diet watchers and the elderly.

F • Hydrogenated oils are disease breeders, harmful to health, and a waste of money. They have very little food value and are said to be aplastic, a potent cause of arteriosclerosis and heart attacks.

F • Aromatize various 8-ounce bottles of oil with various herbs or mixtures of herbs, 1 tablespoonful to each wide-mouthed bottle. Use lemon balm, basil, chamomile, oregano, thyme, citrus peels (orange, etc.), rosemary, mint, marjoram, and any of your favorite herbs and gentle spices. Place on warm oven top, on or next to a warm radiator, or on an ever-warm oil burner (as we do). Let it stay warming 4 to 5 days. Label ingredients.

F • An oil aromatized with dill, basil, mint, or rosemary may be used to season noodles, macaroni, and spaghetti. It is added to the water before boiling. And the oil keeps the water from boiling over, too.

F • Keep the bottles near your stove. Use a pastry brush to brush the oil over broiling and frying foods and baked dishes.

F • Olive oil: kept covered tightly and refrigerated, it will not get rancid. Though the oil will harden, a few minutes at room temperature will return it to liquid form.

M • For an earache: warm olive oil, fill the ear, and plug with absorbent cotton. Do this 3 to 4 times a day.

To remove white spots on furniture rub with a little olive oil. • **H**

When painting, use a small amount of vegetable oil to remove the • **H** splatters from arms and face.

A remedy for a wart: keep it moist with castor oil during the day. • **M** Rub in garlic juice before retiring. Keep covered with Band-aid.

A jiffy remedy for nasal irritation: a few drops of vegetable oil • **M** swabbed in each nostril.

If cold weather makes your skin very dry, apply an edible vege- • **C** table oil or pure lanolin. Gently massage a little of one or both into the skin and wipe off with tissues or absorbent cotton. In a pinch, rub in some cod liver oil.

A "skin oil" made in your kitchen laboratory: blend ½ cup vege- • **C** table oil and 2 egg whites. Massage into face and let it stay on 1 to 2 hours or longer. Before retiring, wash with only a cupful of cold water containing 1 teaspoon of lemon juice. This composition is equally good for those "alligator elbows." Massage them well 3 or 4 times a day.

Ladies: the experts suggest removing *all* your makeup before • **C** going to bed. You must cleanse and rinse every night. An excel- lent and pure cleansing agent is solid vegetable oil. Use a soft cloth, not tissues, to remove the makeup. Then, rinse the face with a mild astringent (for oily skin) such as diluted or straight lemon juice, or a mild freshener such as a strong infusion of herbs (1 teaspoon marjoram and chamomile, ½ teaspoon rosemary and lavender to a cup of hot water) (for dry to normal skin). Removes the last traces of cream and improves circulation.

Castor oil is an excellent remedy for scalp and skin sores. Rub in a • **C** little 3 to 4 times a day, and over all the scalp before a shampoo.

OINTMENT

A commercial cream from my pharmacy years consisted of corn- • **M** starch, castor oil, and zinc oxide powder. Equal parts of the powders were mixed in enough oil to yield a smooth paste, which was applied to skin irritations such as chafing, urine burns and diaper rash of infants.

OKRA

M • Okra's mucilaginous and emollient qualities make it a valuable remedy for irritations of the bronchial and alimentary organs. Place several cut pods (leaves and roots, if available) in a pint of boiling water, ¼ teaspoon each of thyme and mint, cover and simmer 20 minutes. Strain and when cool, add enough honey to sweeten. Take 2 teaspoons every hour or as needed.

ONION

F • The onion is one of the oldest known vegetables, worshipped in ancient Egypt and regarded by the Romans as a god who guarded the kitchen and guided the healing of battle wounds and skin diseases. . . . But the adverse effects must be also regarded: when taken in too large quantities, the raw onion becomes unwholesome and indigestible, and often stays in the stomach 1½ to 2 days before being digested by the gastric juices. In that state, the food is known to cause sharp spasms. However, one may have one or two thin slices of white or red onion with a vegetable salad.

G • The greens of all members of the onion family may be freely taken and a continual supply of their nutrients are yours by cultivating the foods right in your kitchen. With garlic, separate the cloves and press gently into sandy soil. Water well and set aside anywhere in the kitchen. Treat small or sprouted onions, as well as scallions and shallots, the same way. When the scallionlike tops reach a height of 6- to 8-inches, cut close to the white area, wash, and incorporate them into the salad. These greens, cut or diced, go well with cottage or creamed cheese.

F • Need onion juice? Halve a chilled onion and squeeze out the juice with a lemon-orange juicer. Pour into a tightly capped bottle and refrigerate.

84

To prevent tears when cutting or grating an onion, keep it in • **H**
refrigerator for 1 or 2 days before using.
Or peel it under cold water and breathe through the mouth.
Or, a friend informed me, when peeling onions, put a slice of
bread between the teeth until finished.

Onion skins peel off better if a thin slice of the bulb is first • **H**
removed from each end.

To prevent onion breath odor, chew dark green vegetables with • **H**
the onion: parsley, watercress, or spinach. Later, eat an apple.

To remove onion smell from knife and cutting board, rub with • **H**
salt and water, or lemon juice, or with a raw tomato.

The outside brownish peels of yellow and red-skinned onions • **H**
make a good dye source. When included in the water cooking
hard-boiled eggs, they'll yield truly beautifully colored eggs.
Cotton and wool material can be dyed from light yellow to
medium brown (bronze).

To brighten the gold leaf of your picture frames, rub with a warm • **H**
onion or onion juice, then wipe dry.

Clean, mesh onion bags are perfect for remnants and scraps of • **H**
assorted materials. Being able to see through them saves you the
trouble of rummaging through boxes and bags and drawers of
scrap cloth. Also great for holding and hanging suet outside for
the birds.

OPENING LIDS

Having trouble opening a stuck lid? Hot water doesn't open it? • **H**
Nor does tapping it inverted on a hard surface? Tap gently
around the side edges and then the top edges. Hold the lid with a
towel and, pressing it down, turn it with a firm hand or wrap a
rubber band around the lid—it provides some friction. Please
don't copy friend Harry's trick of using a vise to undo a tight lid,
or you, too, will be hurrying to the doctor with a cut hand.

ORANGE

F • To obtain more juice from oranges, let the fruit soak in cold water for a while before squeezing.

F • Grated or powdered, the dried rind serves as excellent seasoning in cakes, pastry, bread, and tea.

H • The rind, coarsely cut and dried, is included in herb sachets.

M • Orange (and lemon) peels enter into an aromatic cordial for stomach disorders, cramps, and the like. Into a pint of hot water, stir a tablespoonful of dried orange peel, 2 teaspoonsful of lemon peel, and 1 teaspoonful of ground (bruised) cloves. Cover and allow to stay covered for 20 to 30 minutes. Strain and take warm-tepid doses of 1 or 2 tablespoonsful every 2 to 3 hours. Refrigerate when not using and warm the liquid when needed.

Be sure that the orange and lemon were organically grown lest you ingest also some of the dangerous (poisonous) chemical used to dye their skins.

H • Want to get rid of strange oven odors? Place a few large peels on the rack and heat at 325° for 10 to 15 minutes.

OVEN

H • To clean a grease-laden oven, place a pan (1 to 2 pints) of hot water and 1 to 2 tablespoonsful of ammonia in the oven and let it stay overnight. Sponge off grease in the morning. Cleans very well and costs a fraction of the price of commercial oven cleaners.

H • To make your oven heat faster, light it and leave it open 2 or 3 minutes. This also prevents condensation and inside rusting.

PANCAKES

F • Keep a whole batch warm as you make more by keeping them between two or three folds of a heavy towel in a warm oven.

PAPAYA

When papaya is in season, try to eat it every day. Not only is it • **M**
highly nutritious, an excellent source of protein, minerals, and
fruit acids, but it also offers many healing, therapeutic values. It
gives almost immediate relief in dyspepsia, indigestion, and
stomach upsets. It removes accumulated mucus and any decayed
and morbid matter from the digestive and intestinal tract. It
provides enzymes not found in most fruits and digests and readies
food for quick assimilation. It cleanses the mouth and teeth and
offsets offensive breath.

PAPER

Those almost dry paper towels used only once to dry your hands • **H**
may be reused for wiping up the usual daily kitchen messes. This
not only is a money saver, but minimizes the constant deposit of
paper in the trash can.

To reduce the waste of paper bags, egg cartons, and wrappings, • **E**
see SHOPPING.

PARSLEY

Parsley is a nutritious and flavorful green. Your young children • **G**
will pick some from the windowsill pot when their appetite sig-
nals a need for leaf nutrients. See HERBS for growing parsley in
your kitchen.

You like garlic but it doesn't like you? It's showing off through • **M**
your breath? Parsley helps mask the aroma. It's best to chew the
uncooked leaves thoroughly.

PASTE

If you've run out of paste, you can make some in your kitchen. • **H**
Take a little flour, add a bit of water, and mix—it should be
thick—and add a pinch of salt, which preserves it. Good recipe for
young children to use because it won't hurt them if eaten.

H • Boiled paste sticks somewhat better:

Add cold water to ½ cup of flour until it's like cream. Simmer for 5 minutes. (Wintergreen or oil of clove will make it smell nice. Or vanilla.) This should be stored in the refrigerator, covered.

PEACHES

F • Nutrition experts now claim that peaches and not apples keep the doctor away. Fresh, unpeeled peaches supply 40 percent fewer calories than apples, almost twice as much vitamin C, and a far greater amount of vitamin A.

PEPPER

M • A *Poison* label should appear on the pepper (and salt) shaker. Pepper disturbs the delicate stomach lining, and can lead to ulcer disturbance and catarrh.

M • Red pepper serves admirably in homemade remedies. A powder of spices (1 ounce pepper and 2 ounces each of mustard and ginger) when mixed with cornmeal or flaxseed and hot water may be applied warm to a bruised area, and its rubifacient warmth relieves or checks the attending pain.

M • My grandfather often prepared a Musterole-type rub by incorporating about a tablespoonful each of powdered pepper and mustard and a little of ginger and cloves in lard, chicken, or mutton fat. A cold or ache or sprain called for a none-too-gentle massage with this hot ointment and then a hot, wet towel, on top of which went the hot water bottle.

H • A good ant repellent: Equal parts of borax and powdered red pepper.

H • Powdered red pepper is a good "warming powder" for ice skaters, walkers, and policemen in winter. Dilute 1 part in 8 or 10 parts of talc and put into the shoes. Try it.

You can prevent your playful puppy from chewing up your house with a pepper treatment. Spray his favorite spots with a little water and put on a tiny bit of red (cayenne) pepper. That'll teach him. • **H**

A circle of black pepper around the base of a flower vase will stop a cat from chewing the flowers. • **H**

PEPPER, SWEET

Green or red, this is the mild, sweet, not hot, variety. The reddish pepper adds a beautiful color to a vegetable salad. On ripening, pepper doubles its vitamin C content. Whenever possible, do eat the red rather than the green kind. • **F**

When preparing vegetable salad, it is best to cut the food in halves (or thirds) lengthwise. Less cutting helps preserve the nutrients. When preparing stuffed peppers, use a curved grapefruit knife to remove the insides and the shell remains undamaged. • **F**

PERFUME

A homemade "perfume" may be easily prepared in the kitchen by making a strong vinegar of your favorite aromatic herbs and spices. Double the quantity of the spices suggested in a recipe and let the herb-spice ingredients blend with the liquid for 3 to 4 weeks. Shake the mixture every day. • **C**

Variations: Use a base of sesame oil or of equal parts of cider vinegar and white wine. When using the oil, it must first be boiled for 20 minutes and allowed to cool. A kind of rose oil has been made in India by steeping rose flowers in the prepared oil. (We have used lemon and other citrus peel, cloves, sandalwood, and orange flowers.) • **C**

A scented powder may be composed of equal parts of every kitchen spice, I am informed, plus orris root equal to the whole amount. • **C**

Queen Elizabeth I compounded her own perfume. She simmered a quantity of marjoram in a syrup (sugar and water) base for a • **C** given time and when this had cooled, added benzoin (benjamin) powder.

PETROLEUM JELLY

C • Solid petrolatum is not recommended as an ointment base. Its only advantage over natural fats (lard or lanolin) is that it does not so readily become rancid. It does not readily penetrate the skin and has been used only when absorption is not desired.

PICKLES AND PICKLING

F • The home pickler will find several sources for items to preserve: at roadside stands (which frequently offer "unsalable" yet quite usable and edible produce); at orchards or by arrangement with supermarket managers. And, why not use the oversupply of some crop in your own garden?

Kitchen pickling is a never-ending challenge and pleasure. It is quite easy to do and a most profitable enterprise. Many of the spicy delicacies ordinarily found in restaurants may be comfortably duplicated in your kitchen-laboratory, and with a minimum of expenditure. Indeed the products of your ingenuity will be far more appreciated by family and friends and, as so often reported to me, will far surpass in taste and quality those of commercial manufacture.

Here is a partial list of possible pickling ingredients:

Vegetables	*Fruits*	*Seasoners*
String bean	Apple	Allspice
Beet	Apricot	Basil
Broccoli stalk	Cantaloupe rind	Celery seed
Cabbage	Cherry	Cinnamon
Carrot	Crab apple	Clove
Cauliflower	Cranberry	Curry powder
Celery (white base)	Currant	Dill
Corn (baby ear)	Gooseberry	Ginger
Cucumber	Grape (green, unripe)	Marjoram
Eggplant	Nasturtium seeds	Mint

90

Vegetables	*Fruits*	*Seasoners*
Mushroom	Nectarine	Mustard seed
Onion	Peach	Oregano
Pepper, red or sweet	Pear	Peppercorn
Pumpkin	Quince	Pickling spice
Salsify root	Tamarind	Thyme
	Tomato (green)	Turmeric
	Watermelon rind	

Our friends leave the spicy liquid in their (store-bought) jars after the pickled cukes and onions, etc., are gone. (One company even claims it isn't their pickles that matter—it's the juice.) Into that liquid go more herbs and spices and the usual cut leftovers such as carrots, cauliflower, celery bottoms, undersized cukes, cabbage, and beets.

When pickling cukes, use the leaves of wild grape vines which are often found growing along roadsides. The leaves add extra tang to cucumber pickles. They should be packed in a crock, one layer of cukes alternately over a layer of leaves, until the container is full. After the pickling solution is added, the whole is weighted down with a heavy stone atop a large inverted plate. Cover the jar with a clean cloth.

Any scum atop pickling liquid is a natural development. A thin sprinkle of powdered mustard will have it settle to the bottom of the jar and will add no extra flavor to the pickles.

Above all, be sure to seal the prepared item in hot, sterilized jars. Store your finished items in a dark cool place, for example, in a corner of the cellar.

In the following recipes, sugar means raw brown, vinegar is cider, wine, or herb, and salt is sea salt. Use your own seasoning tricks. Suggestions: use basil for tomatoes, dill and savory for beans, fennel seed for peaches, lemon balm for fruits, caraway and celery seeds for beets, and the latter two plus juniper berries, savory, and mint for sauerkraut.

Brine: 1½ quarts water, 2 cups vinegar, and ½ cup sea salt. Will pickle 5 pounds of small cukes or small tomatoes.

Jerusalem artichokes: Use 2 quarts of uniform size, previously scrubbed and thoroughly dried, ¾ to 1 pound peeled, sliced onions. Alternate layers of the tubers and onions in jars, pour the hot pickling mixture over them and let stand. The next morning seal with tops.

The pickle: ¾ pint vinegar, 1¼ pound sugar, ½ tablespoon each of mustard powder, seed, and turmeric, 2 ounces salt, and 1 or 2 small red peppers for each jar.

Beets: Boil a pound of them until tender, remove from heat, drain, and when cool, peel them. Boil the pickle for a few minutes to dissolve the sugar; add the beets, again bring the liquid to boiling. Remove from heat and pack while still hot.

The pickle: 2 cups vinegar, 1 cup sugar, and 1 tablespoon mixed pickling spices held in cloth.

Green pepper: Trim and cut 12 into eighths. Bring to a boil 1 quart each of water and vinegar. Add 2 tablespoons sugar, 1 tablespoon vegetable oil, ½ teaspoon salt, and a clove of garlic to each of six jars. Pack the cut peppers into the jars, add the hot vinegar liquid and seal. Let stay at room temperature for 8 to 10 days, each day turning the jars to distribute the flavoring evenly.

Gherkin pickles: Soak about 50 gherkins in ice water, dry, and pack into jars. Add enough cider vinegar to cover, pour it out, and blend it with ½ ounce dry mustard and ½ cup sea salt. Pour the mixture over the gherkins and seal.

Kosher dill pickles or tomatoes: Pack the food (washed and dried) in quart jars, and to each add a clove of garlic, 1 red pepper, 2 or 3 peppercorns, and fresh dill. Add hot brine to fill, and seal.

Dill pickles: Cucumbers, okra, or green cherry tomatoes. Scrub the food clean, pack into quart jars. To each add a sprig of cut dill, 1 pod of red pepper, a clove of garlic. Put a silver knife in the jar, and add hot brine liquid. Withdraw the knife and seal the jar.

The brine: 2 quarts vinegar, 1 quart water, 1 cup salt. This brine will pickle about 1½ gallons of cucumbers.

Turnips: Pack a quart of peeled and cut roots into jars. Pour the liquid cold over them, seal, and let stand for 3 to 4 weeks. Chill before serving.

The pickle: 2 cups vinegar, 1 tablespoon mixed whole spices, 1 clove peeled garlic, a small red pepper, and 1 teaspoon salt.

Zucchini: Slice thin 4 pounds of zucchini and 1 pound of peeled onions, and cover with water in which is dissolved ½ cup salt. Let this stand an hour and drain. Bring the pickle to a boil and cook 3 minutes. Pack hot in 4 sterilized jars and seal.

The pickle: 1 quart vinegar, 2 cups sugar, 2 teaspoons each celery seed, mustard seed and powder, and turmeric.

Crab apples: Bring the pickle to a quick boil, allow to cool and add 2½ pints of uniformly sized apples. Slowly bring to a boil, decrease the heat, and simmer for 5 minutes to prevent breaking of the skins. Remove the pot from the heat, add the spice bag, and let the fruits rest in the syrup overnight. Fill the jars with the apples, over which pour the cold syrup and seal.

The pickle: 1 pint vinegar, 2 cups sugar, ½ cup water, and 2 tablespoons mixed pickling spices tied in cloth.

Peach: Put 4 pounds peeled peaches into a crock, pour the pickling liquid over them, and let stand. The next morning, drain the liquor and bring to a boil. Repeat for 5 days. Cover jar tightly.

The pickle: 1 pint vinegar, 2 pounds sugar, and ¼ ounce each of whole cloves and stick cinnamon.

Watermelon rind: Use the rind of a firm watermelon. Remove green skin and inside pink. Cut the rind into 1-inch squares, place in a pot, cover with boiling water, and boil for 10 to 15 minutes or until tender. Drain and add a pickle containing half the sugar content (reserve the other half). Bring to a boil and pour over the rinds, which you should keep covered with syrup while cooking. Cover and let stand overnight. The next morning, drain the syrup, add the balance of the sugar, and heat to boiling. Stir well and pour the syrup over the rind. The next morning, add diced slices of one lemon and one orange, add to the syrup, and seal hot into sterilized jars.

The pickle: 10 (5 and 5) cups sugar, 2 cups vinegar, ½ teaspoon each of oil of cinnamon and cloves.

Be sure to record all the recipes and the date of preparation.

Your local library offers you many books, whole portions of which pertain specifically to pickling, canning, and preserving. Try a few variations of such recipes as appeal to you, or, using ingredients on hand, try to invent a few new recipes and create new taste-appealing combinations.

Do consult with the home economist at your local County Extension Service.

PLANTS

G • Does gas harm plants in the kitchen?
This may have happened years ago when coal gas was used for cooking or lighting. An "out" pilot could end kitchen (or household) plants. Little danger today. The modern gas stove automatically shuts off when the pilot light goes out. Natural gas is mostly used today in the city and is far less dangerous than coal gas or propane.

Greater danger to one's plants arises from cooking deposits (especially from frying meats) and from using household deodorant sprays (aerosols) to overcome cooking odors.

The following plants are resistant to but not immune to gas: Bromeliads, cacti, succulents, begonias, patience, pick-a-back, English ivy, wax plant, holly fern, rubber plant, sansevieria. (This is only a partial list.)
Resistance will depend on the ventilation, the concentration of the gas, and the time of year. A horticulture expert has stated that artificial gas was injurious to most plants: African violets will not bloom, Jerusalem cherry (a spring house plant) will drop its fruits and leaves, and others will simply look really sick. (See HERBS.)

PLASTIC CONTAINERS

G • That empty half-gallon plastic jug with handle has many uses: Clean thoroughly and dry. Cut off the jug's bottom diagonally, but leave the cap on. Use in the garden to spread mulch, fertilizer, and topsoil. Keep one handy in the car, truck, and back hall to spread sand in winter.

Need a "sitter" for your house plants while you're away for a • **G** weekend or for 2 weeks? They'll stay fresh and healthy if you water each plant thoroughly and cover it with a reusable plastic bag. Fasten the bag around the pot with a plant wire or elastic band. The water that condenses inside the bag will suffice to conserve moisture for the plant while you're away.

Wash your empty bleach jug with warm water and soap, rinse • **H** twice with cold water, and use as a watering can.

A friend cut a bleach jug down to ¼ size as a food dish for her cat.

Transform the bottom half of plastic bleach bottles into other • **H** useful articles: they make an excellent pail for youngsters to use in the sandbox or at the beach. Holes punched on both sides provide space for a shoelace handle.

The pail also becomes a carryall for cleaning material, odds and • **H** ends, paints, and fix-it items. Nail it to the broom closet, garage, or toolshed for a handy, catchall shelf.

Cut in half, a bleach jug has served me as a soil scooper for garden • **G** work.

A good idea for children in wintertime: Not even their two pairs • **H** of mittens will keep out the wetness when they're making snowballs or snowmen or sledding. On top of the first pair, put plastic sandwich bags and follow with the second heavier pair. The bags are flexible and waterproof (and too small to pull over their heads). I find that older children have used bread wrappers cut down to fit their larger hands.

POMEGRANATE

M • An infusion (and concentrate) of dried pomegranate rinds is still much used as a gargle: Boil 2 tablespoons in 1½ pints of water until it reduces to a pint. Use strained and as is for throat irritations and as an application to bleeding gums.

POTATOES

F • If you've made the mistake of boiling potatoes, do save the remaining water. Use it in place of milk in a cake recipe: the cake will keep fresh much longer. The liquor may also be used in soups, stews, casseroles, or marinating mixtures, or as a steaming liquid for other vegetables.

F • To make your baked potatoes a beautiful brown, wash the skins well, dry, and cover with vegetable oil before putting them into the oven. Place them on foil before heating.

F • Hope you'll no longer eat mashed boiled potatoes, which have lost nutrients in peeling and long cooking. Bake or steam them only. Potatoes steamed in their jackets can be mashed. Do use the flat surface of a masher to stir sauces. Prevents scorching and keeps the bottom of the pan clean.

F • Peeled too many potatoes by mistake? Cover with cold water, add a little (brown or cider) vinegar, and refrigerate. They'll keep a few days.

F • Ever eat a potato sliced *raw* in a salad or soup?

G • To keep heather fresh, stick the stems in a raw potato.

M • If you think a potato is just for eating, I've got news for you: A thin slice of salted raw potato rubbed on hives or mosquito bites quickly relieves the itching.

M • For a fresh burn or scald, cut and apply a thin slice of this tuber to ease the pain and take the sting out of the burn.

To remove old and stubborn blackheads: mash a boiled potato • **M**
into a pulp and, while hot, place some on cheesecloth and apply
to the area to be treated. Repeat two or three times to adequately
soften the blackheads and they'll be removed with ease.

Remove vegetable stains from your hands by rubbing with a cut • **H**
raw potato. Rubbed on a painted surface, potato will remove
pencil grease and other tricky spots. Wipe with damp cloth or
sponge.

To clean tarnished silver, soak it in potato water for about 2 • **H**
hours.

POTPOURRIS

Potpourris include herbs and spices whose symphony of scents is • **H**
retained in glass jars. One may include cooking seeds like anise,
coriander, cardamom, and the flowers of hollyhock, roses, and
phlox. Pansies and delphiniums add extra color. The prime
requirement is the addition to the mixture of a few drops of any of
these oils: bergamot, eucalyptus, sassafras, rosemary, neroli,
lemon, or orange. The sachet fixatives apply here (1 ounce to a
quart of rose petals). A moist potpourri is made with alternate
layers of salt and herbs which are heavily weighted down and
stirred occasionally to keep from molding. (See SACHETS.)

PROCESSED FOODS

Man's tampering with everyday foods results in a great loss of • **F**
vitally needed nutrients. Research nutritionists have disclosed
appreciable losses of two essential elements, vitamin B_6 and pantothenic acid, in frozen and canned foods. From 37 to 45 percent
of the vitamin B_6 content of fresh, raw vegetables is lost, as is 37 to
57 percent of pantothenic acid. Canned vegetables show losses of
from 55 to 77 percent of B_6 and 46 to 77 percent of pantothenic
acid. Canned meats, poultry, and fish, from 42 to 49 percent of B_6.
Processed meats, from 50 to 75 percent of both nutrients.
Processed and refined grains, from 51 to 93 percent of B_6 and from
37 to 41 percent of the pantothenic acid.

The refining of flour results in a loss of 50 to 86 percent of seven vitamins.

Mind you, these losses occur long before the consumer buys such foods; more losses take place because of improper cooking. The lesson: eat a maximum of unprocessed and nature-all fresh foods. (See CHEESE.)

PRUNES

E • Prunes, like other dried fruits, should be soaked in cold water until thoroughly soft and eaten in moderation lest the urine's acidity be increased.

Oxalic acid occurs in many foods as *calcium oxalate* but in sorrel, rhubarb, spinach, and prunes there's an inordinate amount. During cooking the free oxalic acid unites with calcium, especially in the markedly decreased alkalinity of the blood, to form stones of calcium oxalate in the kidneys and bladder. This pathological effect coincides with the excessive consumption of such acid-forming foods as meat, cheese, and cereals.

QUINCE

F • Admittedly, this acidulous fruit, even when ripe, is almost totally unpalatable. But the enterprising kitchener considers quince an excellent starting point for the preparation of tart jellies and marmalade. (The latter word is derived from the Portuguese *marmelo,* a quince.)

M • A glycerin-less quince lotion is syruped with raw brown sugar or honey for the usual coughs, and with the addition of a few drops of tincture benzoin compound becomes an effective remedy for a hoarse throat and laryngitis. To each cupful of the glycerin-less liquid, add a cupful of a strained decoction of hoarhound, colts-foot, and thyme (½ teaspoon of each to 1½ cups of hot water.)

C • Quince lotion has for decades been used as a soothing hand lotion, hair-set-and-combing dip, and eye lotion. To prepare a lotion, add a few seeds to a cup of hot water and, when cool, strain. A thicker solution is obtained by cooking the seeds with a few bits of Irish moss, but in both cases, add a little glycerin.

Many years ago, a popular hair pomade (Bandoline) consisted of • **C** quince mucilage and cologne water which both men and women applied to the hair for that sleek ("sheik") look and rich luster.

RADISH

Omit radishes from your salad if your digestion is weak; other- • **F** wise, serve them whole in salad. Do not cut them since by the time they are consumed in their cut state, they may have lost most of their nutrients by oxidation.

Eat the tops as well. When young, the greens may be included • **F** with other salad ingredients. The older greens may be steamed alone or with other vegetables. When steamed, the prickles on the older, larger leaves soften and are not noticed.

RAISINS

They must be soaked in cold water for two reasons: eaten un- • **F** soaked, they may cause stomach cramps because of the sudden absorption of fluid; secondly, to remove chemical preservatives. An excellent between-meal snack for children *and* adults.

REFRIGERATOR

Did you know that freezing changes some flavors? Potency of • **F** onion flavor decreases; that of spices and garlic increases.

A small flat sponge or paper towels kept in your vegetable bin will • **E** absorb most of the excess moisture collecting there. This will prevent spoilage of greens. Wash and dry the sponges every 3 to 4 weeks.

H • To make the rubber seals around your refrigerator or freezer door last longer, wash them with soap and water, dry, and apply talcum powder.

H • The varied refrigerator odors may be absorbed by merely putting a few pieces of charcoal in an open glass jar. Keep the jar in the rear of the refrigerator.
Or use a vanilla-soaked cotton ball in a whiskey glass to do this. Odors are also absorbed by unwrapped slices of lemon.

H • Save empty frozen food boxes. They're just right for sandwiches and will keep them fresh.

H • Take no chances of possible shock. When defrosting, be sure to first pull out the plug from the wall socket.

H • Defrosting the freezer? To speed up, just put a pan of hot water in the freezer. However, be sure that the refrigerator's instruction book does not warn against this practice, and that it does specify which areas are coated with protective material.

When defrosting your freezer, do not add hot water to fill the ice trays. Usually the trays are coated with special protective material and hot water may remove it.

H • One good reason for not putting foods in paper bags in the refrigerator is that paper is porous and often absorbs odors which may be transferred to the stored foods.

RICE

F • Use whole brown rice. By comparison, the white, processed variety offers very few nutrients. An occasional splurge with wild rice really gives one a health lift. Above all, do not waste your money and health on precooked rice.

F • Before heating, allow it to soak in cold water until the water is fully absorbed. Add soaked rice to boiling water, cook 30 minutes at moderate heat, and stir occasionally. Add more water if necessary.

F • Rice may be powdered in a grinder or blender and added to a simmering soup (near end of the cooking) or when you're about to blenderize a portion of the soup. It thickens the soup and enriches it.

Try seasoning rice with ground savory or caraway seeds (½ teaspoonful to a quart of water), or with curry, saffron, or marigold flowers. Let ½ teaspoonful of curry soak in a little warm water 20 to 30 minutes. Do the same with a pinch of Spanish saffron or ¼ teaspoonful of the Mexican variety and stir in slowly. • **F**

Variations in flavor: tomato or other vegetable juice, lemon juice, or wine for part of the water. • **F**

Add color to your rice: to a measured cup of rice, add ⅛ teaspoonful each of curry and paprika. Or add cranberry juice. It yields a very pretty color and characteristic tang. Or add chopped or shredded green pepper, chives, spinach, parsley, or watercress. Saffron or marigolds, for yellow. • **F**

RINDS

The dried rinds of tangerines, oranges, lemons, and limes offer a year-long supply of seasonings for pekoe tea, cake, soups, stews, bread, stuffings, wines, preserves, and fruit punch. Didn't your grandmother use all of these rinds to make marmalade? The rinds also enter into sachets and potpourris. • **F**

The finely ground dried rind of grapefruit has been a chief ingredient of my "cold breaker" remedy (with mint and sage) prepared as a hot infusion. • **M**

For watermelon and cantaloupe rinds, see PICKLES AND PICKLING.

ROSE PETALS

Fresh petals dipped in honey are a delicious and nutritious nibble. • **F**

The petals may also be ground or powdered and mixed into jellies or gelatins as an extra ingredient. • **F**

101

F • East Indians use rose petals to flavor coffee.

G • Did you know that a sugar lump placed in the water will cause rosebuds to open early?

G • Save all rose petals. They can be employed as a hay fever remedy. Steep until cool a level teaspoon of ground petals in a cup of hot water. Filter the liquid through filter paper and insert 2 or 3 drops in each eye 4 or 5 times a day. They may be eaten, or crystallized, and they should always be included in sachets and potpourris. In the latter preparation, use also the dried flowers of lily-of-the-valley, pinks, and violets, and the leaves of pelargoniums.

M • When dried, rose petals have been used as an eye drop or lotion in cases of hay fever. (Ask your druggist about commercial preparations that use them.) They are first steeped in hot water for 10 or 15 minutes. The solution when cool is strained through cotton and then dropped into the eye 4 to 5 times a day.

SACHETS

H • There's no great magic to sachets. The ingredients for sachets and potpourris are right in your cabinets. Use whatever combinations of herbs suit your sense of smell and whichever ingredients are in plentiful supply. Herbs: marjoram, rosemary, thyme, lavender. Spices: cloves, cinnamon, allspice. Use the dried rinds of tangerines, lemons, limes, and especially oranges. Rosebuds, lavender, and marjoram often serve as a base for sachets and constitute about ¼ to ⅓ of the total. A fixative is needed: gum benzoin, orris root, or sweet flag.

H • We have used cloth bags (actually discarded blouse or shirt material) to hold the sachets and these we've hung in closets and between linens. The more colorful silk (but smaller, 4-inch size) bags have served as moth deterrents if placed in the corners of and beneath the seats of upholstered chairs. I can recall my mother and aunts hanging these little aromatic bags over the backs of the parlor chairs.

Aromatic herbs are not only for seasoning foods and for drinking • H
herb teas (tisanes). Their medicinal and tonsorial properties are
well known, as are their valued presence in vegetable gardens as
companion herbs. But dozens of herbs (and spices) that rest on
your shelves are at hand's reach in the flower garden and kitchen,
and others considered weeds may and should become ingredients
of sachets, potpourris, bath bags, and large-sized herb pillows,
and smaller ones (6 × 9 inches) called "tuck-ins." Sachets require
the usual array of cooking herbs: lemon balm, basil, lavender,
marjoram, rosemary, thyme, lemon verbena, and woodruff; and
these spices: allspice, cinnamon, clove, mace, and nutmeg; the
dried rinds of oranges, tangerines, limes, and lemons.

The hops waiting to be brewed and that ever-living scented
geranium are much used not only in tisanes, but in sachets as well.
The garden offers the unopened flower buds of lilacs, the flowers
of heliotrope and lily of the valley, rosebuds, southernwood,
peppermint, spearmint, lemon verbena, and sweet violets. And in
Nature's garden one will find chamomile, sweet clover, sweet
goldenrod, assorted mints, milkweed flowers, and wormwood.

SAGE

E • While we were growing up, sage tea (plain or with other herbs) was our panacea for all external and internal disorders: we used it externally for scratches and insect bites, internally for stomach aches, liver disorders, colds, feverish conditions, and with pennyroyal and motherwort for most "female complaints."

SALAD

F • Start your heavy meal with a large salad of fresh vegetables. The salad satisfies the appetite almost completely and tends to prevent the danger of needless overeating.

F • Please use a minimum of white foods. Lettuce should not be the iceberg type. The greener the better. But it is OK to eat white uncooked cauliflower.

F • When preparing a tossed salad, sprinkle a little vegetable oil over the leaves and toss them some 10 or 15 times to ensure the oil's clinging, the better to seal their surfaces from oxygen. So doing, it is claimed, helps preserve the vitamins and other nutrients.

F • When garlic-juicing the salad bowl, use a piece of bread to press the clove. Prevents smelly fingers.

F • Try preseasoning the bowl with the fresh juice of an onion.

F • Salt should be omitted from salad (and all foods). There is enough sodium and chlorine in every green leaf to provide an ample daily need of salt (sodium chloride).

SALAD DRESSING

F • Here are some interesting dressings for vegetable salads:

1. Sesame or peanut oil
    Honey
    Lemon juice
    Use equal parts. Shake well before using.

2. ¾ cup tomato juice
   1 tablespoon soy or peanut oil
   Juice of ⅓ lemon or 2 teaspoons herb vinegar
   ½ clove crushed garlic
   Shake well before using.

3. 1 cup sour cream
   2 teaspoons celery seed
   2 tablespoons lemon juice
   (or 1 tablespoon herb vinegar)
   Juice of one clove of garlic
   Chill 1 hour before serving to meld the flavor.

4. 1 cup yogurt and 2 tablespoons honey, well whipped
   Add a teaspoon of sesame seeds and
   2 teaspoons of wheat germ.

5. 4 ounces cottage cheese
   Grated rind and juice of ½ lemon
   ½ tablespoon honey
   A sprinkle of cinnamon or herb of your choice.

6. 1 cup vegetable oil
   ½ cup tarragon or cider vinegar
   2 tablespoons honey or raw brown sugar
   1 clove garlic, finely minced
   ½ teaspoon paprika
   ¼ teaspoon each ground oregano and basil

Combine the ingredients in a jar and shake well. Keep in refrigerator until needed and shake well before using.

7. 2 tablespoons vegetable oil
   2 tablespoons cider vinegar
   ½ teaspoon minced parsley
   ¼ teaspoon oregano
   ¼ teaspoon basil
   Optional: pinch of curry

Combine the ingredients in a jar and shake well. Keep in the refrigerator until needed.

SALT

F • Don't use it for internal purposes. It is a most dangerous chemical and should be considered a poison. Too many sick folks are now on salt-free (and spice-free and fat-free) diets. Sodium and chlorine are provided for in a normal diet. Try substituting powdered kelp (seaweed) for salt, alone or combined with powdered dried leaves of carrots, watercress, and your favorite culinary herbs.

F • Even the garlic or onion or celery salts that are available in markets are 99 percent salt or thereabouts, and include only a meager whiff of the corresponding herb or aromatic oil.

F • If you insist on using salt, use sea salt.

F • If a soup is too salty, add a few slices of raw potato. Boil a few minutes and, if still oversalty, repeat the process with fresh potato slices.

H • To use salt as a stain remover, see STAINS.

H • Salt should be liberally—and immediately—sprinkled over an oven or stove spill. When cool, the whole mess is easily scraped up, and the area then washed and wiped with paper towels.

H • Salt has many cleaning uses: alone for silverware; in a paste with vinegar for brass or copper; with lemon juice for brass and other metals; with turpentine to whiten yellowed enamel tubs and washbasins.

SAUCES

F • Always prepare fresh sauces. But remember, an excess will only camouflage the true taste of the prepared food.

The trouble with most commercial or restaurant sauces is that they usually contain such harm-doers as salt (and herb salts which are 99% salt), spices, MSG, distilled white vinegar and white sugar.

Here are some of my favorites:

106

BASIC SAUCE:

2 tablespoons butter
2-3 tablespoons whole
    wheat flour
2 cups milk
1 teaspoon powdered kelp
2 teaspoons herbs, such as
    basil, celery seed, oreg-
    ano, sage, tarragon,
    thyme, and powdered
    onion or garlic.
Optional: dash paprika,
    mustard, or curry

Melt butter and stir in flour, and slowly add milk and other ingredients. Simmer until smooth. You can substitute 1¼ cups of white wine and 1 ounce of cider or herb vinegar for the milk. To make a thin sauce, use less butter and flour.

FISH SAUCES

CREAM SAUCE:

2 tablespoons butter
2 tablespoons whole wheat
    flour
1 cup milk
1 teaspoon thyme
½ teaspoon basil
    (or ½ teaspoon fennel
    seed)
½ teaspoon kelp
    Dash of paprika

Mix the flour well with the melted butter and gradually add the milk. Add the other ingredients.

HERB SAUCE:

3 tablespoons butter
3 tablespoons whole wheat
    flour
1½ tablespoons vegetable
    broth
1 tablespoon chopped
    watercress
1 tablespoon chopped fen-
    nel leaves
1 tablespoon minced
    chives
1 tablespoon chopped
    chervil

¼ cup milk
⅛ teaspoon kelp, mixed
    with
⅛ teaspoon paprika

Melt the butter and stir in flour. Gradually add the vegetable broth, stirring constantly. Boil gently 5-6 minutes. Add other ingredients and stir slowly until hot.

HERB WINE SAUCE:

1 cup white wine
1 tablespoon tarragon
   vinegar
1 tablespoon minced
   tarragon
1 tablespoon minced
   chives
1 tablespoon minced
   dill leaves
1 tablespoon minced
   parsley
3 egg yolks
¼ cup softened butter
2 tablespoons tomato
   paste
½ cup heavy cream

Add the herbs to the warming wine and vinegar, and simmer 15 to 20 minutes, or until half of the liquid remains. Remove from heat and let cool 10 minutes. Strain. Beat in one egg yolk at a time, alternating with ⅓ of butter. Stir in tomato paste and cream, and blend well.

TOMATO SAUCE:

1 cup fresh small tomatoes
½ cup water
2 tablespoons butter
1 slice lemon
½ teaspoon garlic powder
   Dash paprika
½ teaspoon kelp powder
¼ teaspoon thyme

Mix all ingredients except butter and thyme and simmer until tomatoes are very soft. Rub through strainer. Stir in thyme and butter.

HERB MARINADE:

Lemon rind (ground
   dried, or grated fresh)
Minced parsley
Chervil, or other "green
   tarragon vinegar"

Stir the lemon, parsley, and chervil into the vinegar.

To add a new sparkle to your usual fish sauce, incorporate a thin sprinkle of coarsely ground herbs in the early stage of preparation. Your choice: dill or fennel seeds, basil, savory, or tarragon.

LAMB SAUCES

1½ cup stock (vegetable or meat) 1 cup honey 1 tablespoon mint vinegar ½ fresh mint leaf, chopped	Mix the stock and vinegar and heat. Stir in the honey, add mint and simmer 5 minutes. Variation: Add ¼ teaspoon grated orange peel.

Juice of ½ lemon 1 tablespoon honey 1 teaspoon ground mint ½ to 1 teaspoon lemon rind	Mix together the lemon and honey. Add the mint and lemon rind and blend.

STEAK SAUCE

2 tablespoons margarine 1 small onion, minced 3 ounces garlic or herb vinegar 1 cup water ½ cup minced celery ½ cup minced parsley ½ teaspoon oregano ¼ teaspoon basil ¼ teaspoon celery seed Dash garlic powder ½ cup vegetable oil ½ cup catsup	Melt the margarine over medium heat, add the onion and simmer 3 minutes. Then stir in the liquids. Add the celery and parsley and seasonings to the liquid and blend well. Reduce heat and simmer 25 minutes. Serve hot with roasts, too.

OTHER MEAT AND POULTRY SAUCES

2 ounces margarine
¼ teaspoon minced fresh parsley
¼ teaspoon minced fresh chives
½ teaspoon minced fennel leaves
2 tablespoons minced celery leaves
½ teaspoon ground thyme
½ teaspoon ground marjoram
¼ teaspoon ground sage
2 ounces vegetable oil
1 ounce white wine or cider vinegar

Melt the margarine, and sauté the parsley and chives gently for 3 minutes. Add the fennel and celery and herbs, add the wine or vinegar and simmer 10 minutes. Blend in the oil, stirring well.

1	cup white dry wine	Bring the wine and vinegar to a quick boil and add the herb and greens. Simmer 20 minutes or until liquid is reduced to half amount. Remove from heat, allow to cool and strain into a double boiler. Beat in one egg yolk alternately with ⅓ of margarine, then the tomato paste. Blend well. For veal and poultry.
1	tablespoon tarragon or basil vinegar	
½	teaspoon tarragon	
1	tablespoon minced chives	
1	tablespoon minced scallions	
3	egg yolks	
½	cup margarine	
2	tablespoons tomato paste	

VEGETABLE SAUCES

¾	cup sour cream	Incorporate the egg yolks with the sour cream and add the vinegar. Place the mixture in the top of a double boiler and heat until thickened, stirring constantly.
2	egg yolks	
2	teaspoons tarragon vinegar (or other herb vinegar)	
¼	teaspoon savory	
⅛	teaspoon basil	

1	tablespoon butter	Simmer the chives and chervil in the melted butter a few minutes. Add flour until smooth and cook for 3 minutes. Add the herbs and cook until thick and smooth. Stir in well the lemon juice and remove.
2	tablespoons flour	
2	teaspoons lemon juice	
¼	tablespoon chopped chives	
¼	tablespoon chopped chervil	
¼	teaspoon combined herbs (marjoram, basil or oregano)	

½	cup butter	Mix well and heat the butter, egg yolks, and lemon juice in a double boiler until mixture thickens. Slowly add the hot (boiling) stock and keep beating. Cook the mixture gently for 20 minutes or until the consistency is of soft custard.
	Juice of ½ lemon	
3	egg yolks	
½	cup hot vegetable stock	
⅛	teaspoon each of 3 herbs (rosemary, oregano, basil, marjoram, or thyme)	

Tomato soup or juice may be used as a base for any herb sauce. Stir well ¼ teaspoonful each of thyme and rosemary, plus 1 teaspoonful of minced greens.

(See also HORSERADISH, MAYONNAISE, SALAD DRESSINGS.)

SAVORY

Savory is the perfect flavoring herb for all the bean-pea-lentil   • **F** group and for nonvegetable proteins, such as baked or broiled fish, lamb, veal, meat loaf, egg dishes, and cheese spreads.

SCALLIONS

The greens are preferably eaten uncooked, in a salad. They don't   • **F** like you? Cut them into 1-inch lengths and mix them into a soup or stew.

Use them as a strongly flavored substitute for chives or leeks. Low   • **F** in calorie count, scallions are good for reducers.

The chlorophyllated greens are far more nutritious than the bulbs   • **G** and the bulbs can be replanted. Properly cultivated in a pot of sandy soil, the root bases will produce more and more edible, nourishing , green shoots.

SEEDS

Dry the seeds of squash and pumpkin. Roast them for an en-   • **F** joyable nibble.

The inner seed-meats of peach and apricot are nutritious. The   • **F** "sudden death" prejudice against eating peach and apricot seed-meats was recently raised re eating apple seeds, because they contain a supposedly toxic substance, hydrocyanic acid (or amygdalin). But it also exists in plums, cherries, wild cherries, and elderberries. So, we don't eat these luscious fruits? The important part of the apple is the skin and seed white. Thus, the substance is non-toxic if one eats the seeds with the fruit and not alone. It is a source of nitrilosides or B_{17}, a possible anti-cancer vitamin in incipient cancer. Called laetrile, it has been the source of much controversy.

111

F • There's gold and good food in those innumerable squash and pumpkin seeds folks usually discard. Remove adhering food particles with a brisk washing of cold water, dry, place in a lightly oiled flat tin over a warm radiator or stove, or in a moderate oven for 5 minutes. When thoroughly dry, store in a glass jar. They make an excellent nibble during the winter months. They have a flavor of their own and should not be salted.

E • Peach and plum seeds and cherry pits are good for children's beanbags.

SESAME SEED

F • Buy whole seeds. When "ground" or "freshly powdered" are needed, put them through a coffee grinder or blender. The recently ground seeds will fill a larger measure than whole seeds.

Whole: use as a topping for bread, cake and pastries, soups and stews, poultry stuffing.

Ground: use as an ingredient of bread, rolls, and various pastries. May be included in hot cereal. When used with soup, sprinkle a little over the soup just before it is to be eaten.

SHALLOTS

F • In France this delicious food is used as an everyday source of "greens" for salads, soups, sauces, and spreads, and of course, as a worthy substitute for chives and onions.

G • Early in summer, do purchase a box of shallot bulbs and grow your own greens. The bulbs offer a more delicate flavor than onion, but why not use the mineral-packed greens and reuse the bulbs to grow more greens?

SHAMPOOS (DRY)

C • Need a dry shampoo? Here is a "depression" recipe that was much in vogue several decades ago among housewives who had a cold, couldn't afford the time for a wet shampoo, or just couldn't afford the store-bought item. Mix equal parts of sodium bicarbonate—soda or saleratus to our grandfolks—and corn or other edible starch. (Alone, the latter provides an excellent means of absorbing excessive or annoying secretions, and so may also be used as a dusting powder for infants.) Add a few drops of perfume or toilet water and mix.

Chamomile flowers,from which you can brew a healthful substitute for tea, are similarly used. Powder the dried flowers in a coffee or spice grinder, sift the powder, and use either alone or combined with an equal portion of the above soda-cornstarch powder. The finished products are vigorously rubbed into the hair and scalp, which are then thoroughly brushed. Alone, the chamomile also adds a brightening highlight to the hair but leaves unchanged the natural color of the hair. • C

The following solution may be applied to hair that is faded, dull, or graying. The herbal ingredients are food seasoners and quite likely are on your spice shelf. Simmer for 20 minutes (do not boil) 1 tablespoon of dried rosemary and chamomile flowers and 2 tablespoons of sage. Use the strained solution as a rinse following a shampoo. Allow to dry slowly, and brush well. • C

AFTER-SHAVE LOTIONS

During the last year of World War I—I was then about 11 or 12—I was employed at Feldman's Drugstore. Pay was 75¢ a week and included a free ice cream soda or cone every day. I helped "Doc" Feldman prepare syrups for the soda fountain, various medicinal powders and liquids, and especially store-brand cosmetic formulas. We made bulk quantities of skin and hand lotions, face and body powders, smelling salts, shampoos, wave sets, brilliantines, and other "beauty aids." When 40 years ago I began to operate my own pharmacy, I used similar formulas. • C

Druggist Feldman's favorite after-shave lotion was a thin mucilage (jelly) of quince seeds or Irish moss diluted with bay rum. But I prefer and still use Grandfather's recipe—a little more work and perhaps a better product: To a pint of bay rum contained in a wide-mouthed, oversized bottle, add a heaping tablespoonful each of ground dried peels or orange, lemon, tangerine, and/or lime (at least 3 tablespoonsful). Stir and place in the summer sun or, in the wintertime, near the kitchen stove or

113

radiator, or atop the oil burner. Fit the cover loosely. Stir gently each day and on the third day strain the liquid, replace, and add an ounce or 2 of witch hazel. Grandfather prepared his own witch hazel with witch hazel twigs.

Variations:
- Add 3 drops of any of these oils: clove, wintergreen, cinnamon, and lavender to 14 ounces of bay rum and 2 ounces of witch hazel. Add 1 teaspoonful of glycerin.
- Pour 6 ounces (or small cupful) of cold, boiled water into a wide-mouthed pint bottle and add ½ ounce of rosewater concentrate (obtained at your pharmacy) and a cupful of rum. Stir well and add a cupful of ground, dried rose petals. Allow to sit for 4 or 5 days in a warm area, shake daily, and strain. Add ½ teaspoonful of boric acid, 2 tablespoonsful of glycerin, and enough bay rum to fill the bottle.
- Strain your most flavorful herb vinegar into an equal part of witch hazel.

During the Great Depression, a "toilet vinegar" consisting of aromatic herb oils, alcohol, and diluted acetic acid (vinegar) was sold in drugstores as a toilet water. Doc Feldman called it *acetum odoratum*. This concoction was Grandfather's favorite toilet water for his daughters and their mates. The vinegar was homemade. Actually it was a purposely soured wine, whose chief brewing ingredients were local weedy plants. It was aromatized with seasoning herbs and spices. The witch hazel (he called it *hamamelis*, its Latin version) was a crude distillation of a mash of its ground leaves and twigs and hot water.

These preparations serve well as after-shave lotions, as skin refresheners, and as applications to insect bites, beestings, and scratches.

SHOPPING

E • "Waste not, want not." Fight ever-increasing inflationary food costs! Do practice self-control at the supermarket where every customer is a supermark for dollars easily lost on needless, valueless edibles. Retailers believe that at least 70 percent of their goods are bought on impulse. Make a list of only the items you must replace and buy only them. If you tend to be too self-indulgent, send one of the children with your buying list.

Plan to buy your groceries over the weekend. Thrift sales usually begin on Thursday. Take advantage of weekly specials and markdowns of seasonal products. But watch those weekend food "specials." Are they really money savers or just come-ons? Do the stores offering these good buys also offer lowest prices on most other food?

And when new products—staples of your choice—are being heavily promoted at introductory prices as "loss leaders," then stock up. But beware of the nonspecials located in the vicinity of the advertised foods. If your supermarket is offering specials at near-wholesale prices just to get you into the store, then buy only them, if you need them, and leave. Compare the prices of markdowns or specials displayed near the check-out counter with those of competitive brands found in usual places.

Use your 7¢- and 10¢-off coupons. This economy may reduce your food costs by as much as 6 percent. The market's house brands are generally 12 to 15 percent cheaper than comparable advertised brands. They are often the same product but with the house-brand label. Check the label, however. Sometimes they use more chemical substitutes, food coloring, and preservatives. Then, they are no bargain!

Of several ways to stretch your food dollar, one is to measure the cost and desirability of home-prepared foods compared with convenience foods. Biscuits, pastry, and bread baked in your kitchen will save ½ to ⅔ of the price of such store-bought items. Dehydrated mashed potatoes (4 ounces) cost nearly twice as much as fresh (and offer far fewer nutrients than the original).

Greater savings depend upon your will (or won't) power to abstain from buying nutritionally inferior convenience foods — canned, premixed, frozen, and other man-processed make-believers. With food costs reaching a record high, one cannot afford such extravagance as frozen chicken and turkey dinners, pizza, brown-and-serve rolls and pastry, frozen broccoli and other vegetables, precooked rice, and so on.

Always read the label of every food package before you buy it, right in the market. It's too late when you arrive home with your purchases. If any one of the ingredients confuses you in the least bit, ask the state and federal Food and Drug Administrations to clarify.

To better evaluate many buying pointers, the enterprising and knowledgeable shopper will study carefully the various government bulletins offered free by your local County Extension Service and will especially read health-oriented books. (Many of these are paperbacks.) Or contact the food columnists and home economists of your paper. Yes, do ask your vegetarian friends and the "food nuts" about the qualities of various foods. You'll be pleasantly surprised by their factual and informative answers.

Be a true recycler: You've already been composting leaves, grass cuttings, and your kitchen scraps, but from now on buy drinks in returnable bottles where and when available, return egg cartons, have your store-bought items placed in a box and refuse excess paper bags. Suggest to your market manager that fruits, vegetables, and other foods be sold unwrapped. This eliminates storing and disposing of more bags and cartons and wrappings. And if you buy only what you can use in the next 2 or 3 days, you'll save money by consuming less.

SINK

H • Standing at the sink on a hooked rug or heavy mat makes the sink chores much easier.

116

Can't remove those yellow spots from sink or dishes? Try this easy • **H**
way: if salt does not work, sprinkle a small amount of cream of
tartar and rub the particular area with a halved lemon, juice side
down. Very good if you're in a hard water area.

If your sink is stainless steel and must be cleaned frequently, • **H**
indeed, after each use, wash with hot water and a small quantity
of detergent, using a sponge or cloth. But for small spots, apply
sodium bicarbonate (baking soda) or a mild, nonabrasive soap
powder. Never use steel wool or scouring pads on your stainless
steel sink.

Residents of northern states should flush out their sink pipes at • **H**
least once a month during the cold winter months to prevent
possible clogging due to ice formation and needless plumbing
expense. Simply put a small amount of lye into the pipe and
follow with 2 or 3 gallons of hot water.

To clear a sink or basin drain, try using ½ cup of salt followed by • **H**
boiling water. A slow-draining sink or basin calls for 2 to 3
tablespoonsful of salt and ⅓ to ½ cup of vinegar. Allow to rest a
few minutes and follow with hot water. In 1 hour, treat again with
salt.

To disinfect a sink, clean with a hot solution of salt. Saves on • **H**
scouring powder and bleach.

Keep the sink pipe dry and thus free of insects by ringing it with • **II**
powdered charcoal.

Cover a regular-sized (12-ounce) can with adhesive-backed vinyl • **H**
and keep near sink. A good way of soaking the silverware while
doing the dishes.

To help a very young child distinguish between the hot and cold • **E**
water, mark the respective faucets with red and green adhesive
tape.

SOAP

To make yours last longer, unwrap your soap and allow it to dry • **H** out completely—or "age"—at least 1 month before using.

H • Save all your soap scraps. Put them into a cloth bag or nylon net. Either container is most suitable for the bath or shower, being quite preferable to the usually slippery soap bars.

H • Accumulate soap scraps in a wide-mouth jar. When half full, add hot water to cover and stir. Or you may simmer a panful of the soap with water until a thick mass is formed. The longer the boiling, the thicker it gets. The jelly-like substance may be given to children when taking a bath or used for cleaning or laundering.

H • To yield new cakes, the jellied soap can be poured into molds of aluminum foil or cardboard, or into a square pan, and when well thickened and cool, cut into squares. The soap dries in about two weeks. You not only participate in the economy drive, you've prepared an excellent bath soap and cut down your soap cost.

H • Use an unwrapped bar of soap to impart a sweet-smelling aroma to stored luggage, a dresser drawer, or put under upholstery cushions.

E • An artistically inclined young man I know collected enough left-over soap pieces over a year's time to yield a solid cake of 12 by 24 inches. From this he sculptured a piece of lasting beauty.

SOAP PADS

H • Prevent your soap-filled scouring pad from rusting. Place it in a wide-mouth glass jar and cover with soap-thickened water (or with diluted liquid detergent). The next day you'll have a soft, soapy pad that will work faster and require less hot water to do the work. After scouring a pan, quickly rinse the pad under the hot faucet and replace the clean pad in the jar.

SODIUM BICARBONATE (OR BAKING SODA, SODA)

M • A solution of bicarbonate of soda, 4 tablespoonsful to 8–10 ounces of water, applied locally, relieves the pain of sunburn.

H • Sodium bicarbonate can be used in many of the same ways salt

118

can, but it makes a smoother solution (and paste, if needed).

When a quick dip for crystal glassware or silverware is needed, • **H**
prepare a solution of the powder in tepid-cool water (1 level
tablespoonful to a quart) and brush with a soft toothbrush. Very
good for glass coffee makers and thermos jugs.

Use a stronger solution to clean your stainless steel sink, the • **H**
refrigerator, plastic counters, tabletops, and bathroom tile. It will
also remove stains from china and enameled cookware.

To clean a greasy pan easily, add 1 or 2 teaspoons of soda to the • **H**
water in which it is soaking. Why not use this nonpolluting and
nonenzyme soak for a sinkful of dishes?

Fingers smelling of garlic or onions? Rub them thoroughly in a • **H**
thin paste of soda and water, and rinse with warm water.

Emergency fire extinguisher: if a greasy pan catches on fire, turn • **H**
the heat off and try to cover the pan. Spread a good dose of the
powdered soda over the fire. (An oven fire is quickly extinguished
by merely closing the door after shutting off the heat.) Fill a large
coffee can with the powder and keep handy.

To remove recent grease spots from your dining room carpet, first • **H**
sop up the liquid with a sponge, then rub a liberal amount of the
soda into the spot. Let it be absorbed overnight. Next day, remove
the excess and vacuum the area.

There are many good uses for this chemical, but it must not be • **E**
employed for internal purposes. It has long been rejected as a
remedy for stomach distress or urinary disorders. It may be considered a gargle, or mouth and nose wash. A teaspoon dissolved in
½ glass of water, it is claimed, leaves the mouth feeling "clean and
fresh." Some even use it as a toothpowder.

SOUP

The ingredients: leftover vegetables; celery bases; carrot greens; • **F**
discards from roast, steak, and chops; bones, especially from
shoulder and ends of beef ribs. Thanksgiving's turkey bones also
make good stock.

—Always add parsley or other deep green vegetable leaves.

—Season with herbs, thyme, and marjoram (or others of your choice), ½ teaspoonful of each to a quart of stock.

—Try *not* dosing the mixture with salt. A pinch or two at most.

—Prepare a soup in small quantities.

—Cut fowl or chicken will shorten cooking time of soup.

—Simmer at low heat.

—Keep the lid tightly closed.

—To remove fat from still warm soup, pour the liquid through a colander lined with a clean cloth which has been rinsed in ice cold water.

—Better way to remove more fat: allow soup to cool and skim the solidified fat off the top.

—Once the fat is removed and the soup is cool, freeze in ice cube trays for storage.

—Use your blender to quickly prepare a puree type: when a vegetable soup is finished, blend about ⅓ of a quart measure of soup, or 3 cupsful, for several seconds, replace in pot, and stir.

F • When serving soup, have on hand powdered buckwheat groats, rice, soybeans, and sesame seeds to be consumed with the soup.

F • Use clear, meatless soup stock for preparing rice, macaroni, noodles, gravy, sauce, stew, and casserole dishes. Use it also as a marinade and basting solution.

F • Having prepared a cold soup, into each plateful sprinkle a thin layer of finely cut or minced parsley, spinach, watercress, chervil, dill leaves, or mint. Add a little less of cut leaf tops of onion, scallions, or garlic, and a touch of finely ground lemon rind.

F • Be sure to add 1 tablespoonful of sour cream to each serving of cold beet or spinach soup.

SOUR MILK

F • If you need sour milk in a hurry, stir a tablespoon of lemon juice or cider vinegar into a cupful of sweet milk and let stand a few minutes.

SPICES

Resolve to use the barest minimum of salt and harsh spices such • **F**
as pepper and mustard. They unbalance the digestive juices,
irritate the stomach lining, and sometimes lead to intestinal catarrh and ulcers. Replace these nonessentials with pleasantly
flavored, gentle herbs, such as marjoram, thyme, and savory.

The addition of salt and pepper, or relish, catsup, or pickles to any • **F**
food is an insult to a cook who has already seasoned his or her
preparations.

SPROUTS

In the search for natural, unpoisoned, and unrefined foods, one • **F**
discovers the wonderful world of sprouts, those remarkable health
and dollar savers. Whereas only until recently they were labeled
"faddist," today they rank high among the healthiest of health
foods and are sold as an acceptable article of diet, not only in
health or natural food stores but in local supermarkets.

For thousands of years, the people of China, India, and other
Eastern countries have depended upon these high-powered,
life-sustaining natural vitamins. They have lived well on soy and
mung sprouts and some rice.

In the early 1780s, Britain's admiralty, which realized the importance of (vitamin-C-rich) greens in the daily diet of its navy
men, also introduced the sprouting or germination of grains
aboard ship to prevent crippling scurvy.

With seeds, sink water, and a little patience, you, too, can do
sprouting in your kitchen area. Sprouting is an exciting and
educational process and easy to do.

First, buy organically grown seeds at a local health-food store.
Grains: corn, oats, wheat, rye, rice, millet, barley. Beans and peas:
soya, mung, lentils, fava, pinto, and kidney beans, garden peas,
chick-peas. Seeds: alfalfa, fenugreek, cress, sunflower, radish, and
sesame.

IMPORTANT: Use only dry, unhulled seeds or beans intended for
food. Use none commercially treated for planting, as they may be

coated with poisonous chemicals.

Various receptacles, both commercial and those found at home, may be used for sprout production: unglazed flowerpot or saucer, earthenware bean pot, glass jar, colander, shallow dish, canning jar, tea strainer, and sponge.

The method: use small amounts of dried seeds or beans at a time. A tablespoonful will swell to double its size after soaking and 4 times that after sprouting. Soak the seeds overnight. (Starting amounts may be increased as success appears.) Drain off all the water, place the seeds in a container, and cover loosely since sprouts need air to grow. Rewash beans and peas during the day. The moistened sprouts, kept warm and dark—the kitchen cupboard will do—will sprout in 3 to 4 days. When alfalfa, beans, lentils, peas, and other sprouts (except wheat) are 1 inch high or more, they're ready to eat. Remove and rinse them with cold water, serve, and refrigerate the balance.

My three favorite containers:

THE COLANDER

In it place a white paper towel or cheesecloth on which to soak seeds. The next morning cover with more towel, and soak well by running cold water through the towels. The next day, repeat the soaking and moisten each morning until the sprouts develop. Good for beans and large seeds and grains.

UNGLAZED FLOWERPOT SAUCERS

This container is suitable for alfalfa, radish, wheat, and other small seeds. Let the saucers soak in water a few minutes. Place the moistened seeds in one saucer, cover with a second, and place in a shallow (cake) pan or cooking pot.

Wash and drain enough seeds to cover the bottom, cover the top with cheesecloth, and bind securely with a rubber band. After each rinsing of sprouts, invert the jar to allow thorough draining. (For alfalfa, use 1 tablespoonful of seed and cover with 2 inches of water. You can even drink the drained water.) A glass jar must be kept in the dark.

Notes: when alfalfa sprouts are 1 inch long, they may be exposed to sunlight. The tiny leaves which will appear add vitamin C, chlorophyllated material, and extra taste.
Sunflower seed sprouting should be stopped when the sprouts emerge from the seeds. Eat the sprouts in a day or two, unless you don't mind a bitterish taste.
During the germinating process, the starches of beans are turned into a sugar that provides a source of high body energy. The sprouts develop remarkably high amounts of vitamins B, C, and E, more so than lettuce or celery. Beans lose their gas-producing quality. Make these your source of natural vitamins.

Sprouts are taken in dozens of ways: eat them raw, in salad, blended with other foods, in soups, stews, and casseroles, in sandwiches, meat or fish loaves, and in omelets. Include them in bread and muffin batter.

STAINS

Tea or coffee stains in a cup? Wet with vinegar. Rub with a damp cloth dipped in salt. • **H**

To remove a cigarette stain or any other stain from china or ceramics, apply wet salt with a cork or cloth and rub gently. • **H**

If the wallpaper behind your stove gets spattered with grease, blot the grease with a blotter and apply a warm iron. • **H**

To remove grease stains, make a solution of ½ teaspoon salt and 2 tablespoons alcohol or 1 teaspoon salt and 1 tablespoon ammonia. It will render excellent service. • **H**

H • Sometimes you can remove a grease stain from wallpaper with a paste of cornstarch and cleaning fluid. Let the paste dry, then brush it off.

H • To clean candle stains: wipe with alcohol.

H • If the tube of your percolator gets dirty, percolate salted water through it, about 3 or 4 tablespoonsful for 10 minutes.

H • Did you know that a grease spot on washable clothes is quickly removed by rubbing the spot with detergent to which a few drops of vinegar have been added? Or cover the spot with flour and wait a few minutes. Brush briskly and wash. And chewing gum can be "frozen" with an ice cube until the gum hardens. Scrape off. Soften the remaining gum by pressing in some egg white. Repeat if necessary before washing.

H • Meat and chocolate stains: Use cold water and detergent to remove the excess. Rinse the spot thoroughly and let dry. Sponge any remaining part with a cleaning fluid. If necessary, apply a little bleach to the dried material.

H • Mayonnaise stain: Rub a little liquid detergent in and rinse with hot water. Let dry and use a cleaning fluid if necessary.

H • Wine stain: Sop up the spill. Sprinkle with salt at once, let stand a few minutes, and pour boiling water through the stained portion. A neighbor of mine boils the stain in milk.

H • Remove stains of perspiration, blood, or wine from washable clothing by soaking it in a salt solution before washing.

H • Oil and soot stains on a carpet should be rubbed with salt, then brushed briskly or vacuumed. Repeat if necessary.

(See also SALT, SINKS, and SODIUM BICARBONATE.)

STICKY FRUITS

H • To make easier cutting of sticky fruits like dates, figs, or those used in fruitcake, gently heat the knife, or dip it in warm water.

STORAGE

Storage helps come in various forms. Place a plastic foam egg •   **H**
carton in the kitchen or bureau drawer for storing those countless
odds and ends. The top of the carton may hold combs and emery
boards, files, hand creams, etc.

Similarly, the plastic containers that manicotti comes in provide •   **H**
12 dividers which are excellent for storing, especially for small
items.

Plastic-covered, see-through shoe storage boxes provide excellent •   **H**
storage for floppy, irregularly shaped bags of macaroni, dry
beans, split peas, or soup mixes. Tightly tie each bag before fitting
it into a box. The bags are protected from rough handling and
from possible puncture, and the foods from insects. Also, the
boxes are easy to stack.

That empty six-pack carton will hold boxes of waxed paper, •   **H**
sandwich bags, plastic wrap, assorted sizes of gift-wrapping
paper, etc.

Hang an onion bag on the kitchen closet door. This is a handy •   **H**
place for dirty washcloths, dish towels, and potholders until
washday arrives. Better than tossing damp towels and facecloths
into the hamper.

STOVES

To clean around the knobs and nameplates on your kitchen •   **H**
range, use an old toothbrush and soapsuds.

To remove the yellow from your stainless steel stove, first apply •   **H**
ammonia and let dry. Next a good wash with soap and water and,
after it is wiped dry, a light massage with baby oil.

STRAWBERRIES

Strawberries dissolve tartarous formations on the teeth. This fruit •   **M**
dentifrice greatly helps to prevent dental tartar if a halved berry is

rubbed over the teeth and its juice allowed to stay there for a minute or so before rinsing.

SUGAR

F • The only sugar that should be eaten is the raw, brown kind, never the white, which is without any nutritional benefits. Regular brown sugar is as bad and as unnutritious as white: it is simply refined sugar with some (processed) molasses replaced.

F • Consider sugar one of your white enemies; others are salt, white vinegar, pasteurized milk, and flour. Use either raw brown sugar or, better, honey, or, best, now sweetening (unless baking or canning). White sugar is a major contributing factor in many of our civilization's degenerative diseases, such as heart disease and diabetes. "Pure white" sugar means that the food is devoid of the nutritives required by the body, but high in calories.

H • Brown sugar will keep soft if first removed from the package, transferred to a dry glass jar, and before the lid is closed, a large, fresh peel of lemon, orange, or grapefruit is inserted. Occasionally replace the dried peel with a fresh one. Refrigeration is not necessary. Or store the package in a tightly closed plastic bag in the refrigerator.

SUNFLOWER SEEDS

F • An excellent nibble instead of candy. Cheaper to buy them hulled, saves wear and tear on the teeth. Italian and Armenian markets carry them, as do health food stores.

F • On a reducing or fat-free diet, eat sunflower seeds instead of fatty fish or meats.

F • Good for your caged birds as well. The seeds offer 10 major minerals, many amino acids (they contain 48 percent protein matter), and all the vitamins and protective factors required for overall body health.

126

TARRAGON

Tarragon, "little dragon," is a member of the wormwood family, • F
and though its aromatic leaves are used as herein described, their
taste, in spite of its aniselike flavor, is slightly astringent and
peculiarly strong—almost pungent (like sage). Thus one must be
cautious when using tarragon. It must be judiciously incorporated in salads, sauces, and elsewhere. "If a chance leaf finds its
way into a bunch of Sweet Herbs used for soup, great consterna-
tion will result at dinner-time," according to Frances Bardswell in
her book *The Herb Garden*. Like sage and rosemary, use only ¼
teaspoon for 4 servings; tarragon is rarely used alone—use a pinch
to avoid getting a punch.

TARRAGON VINEGAR

The kitchen uses of tarragon vinegar are usually confined to fish • M
or tartar sauce, salad, or French dressings, but there are other
applications: First, the vinegar is good for insect bites and
beestings.

Equal parts of that vinegar, witch hazel, and turpentine become a • M
liniment for sore spots, bruises, and mild sprains.

To prepare a jiffy and effective gargle, simmer a teaspoonful of • M
sumac berries for 5 minutes in a cup of equal parts of tarragon
and sage vinegars. Strain, mix with an equal part each of honey
and water. Gargle tepid-warm every hour as needed.

Diluted with three parts of sage or rosemary vinegar, tarragon • C
vinegar is used as a post-shampoo rinse to add luster to dull hair.

TEA

Save the once-used bags for future use. They provide a quick • M
remedy for minor burns and hot-water scald: Boil 2 bags vigor-

ously in 8 to 10 ounces of hot water. Allow the solution to cool and apply as a compress. The same cool solution is now recommended by dentists for bleeding gums.

M • A weak, almost colorless infusion of tea (aided by the addition of rose petals) has long been used as an eye drop to relieve the discomforts of hay fever.

M • The universal poison antidote contains toast (or charcoal), milk of magnesia, and tea, whose tannic acid checks alkaline poisons.

M • "Tea for Two" is the reality for tired or puffy eyes. Chill and moisten thoroughly several used tea bags. Lie down, close your eyes, and place the bags on the eyes for 10 minutes. Does wonders!

THYME

M • Although used mostly to season fish and fish chowder, omelets, meats, poultry, and various vegetables, its medicinal values should not be overlooked. A well-known cough syrup once consisted of a sweetened extract of thyme which, as a druggist, I found most helpful in all kinds of coughs and bronchial troubles. Make your own syrup by simmering 1 tablespoonful of thyme in a pint of hot water for 15 minutes; strain the liquid and add enough raw brown sugar or honey to make a syrup. My Herbal Cough Syrup contained Irish moss, boneset, thyme, hoarhound, chestnut leaves, and licorice, and these ingredients may also be used to prepare a cough syrup. In either case, sip 2 teaspoonfuls every ½ to 1 hour as needed.

A tea of thyme, catnip, mint, and fennel (1 heaping teaspoonful • **M**
to a cup of hot water) quickly soothes an upset stomach.

Going to fumigate the kitchen? Remember that this herb's der- • **H**
ivation is from a Greek word denoting an incense to perfume the
temples. Stir a small handful in a pot of hot water and place it on
a warm radiator or on the lowest heat.

Include thyme in your sachets. • **H**

TISANES (OR HERB TEAS)

You may have come across the words *decoction, infusion,* and *tisane,* • **F**
used as alternatives for *tea.* Specifically, a *decoction* is made by
boiling a substance to extract flavor (and nutrients). Preparation
of birch bark is an example. An infusion is a drink made by
soaking or steeping a substance in hot water, as tea and most
herbs are prepared. Tisane was originally applied to barley water,
a decoction. The word is often used, however, to cover all herb
teas, decoctions, and infusions.

Ever take in top cuttings of your ornamental New Jersey Tea? Do • **G**
make use of the dried downy leaves and the flowers of this rather
hardy 4- to 5-foot shrub. During the Revolution and the Civil
War, those plant parts served as a substitute for the imported tea.
Interesting that the leaves give to hot water green color and a
taste similar to that of green tea.

Medical compendia state that an alcoholic solution called
ceanothyn has been employed to increase the coagulability of the
blood, while the plant itself is believed of good value in problems
of blood circulation.

You can prepare a tea by stirring well 1 teaspoonful of the coarsely ground, dried parts in a cup of hot water and covering for 10 to 15 minutes. Stir and strain. Sweeten with a little honey if necessary, or add extra flavoring with the dried peels of orange, lemon, or tangerine. Sip slowly and enjoy.

TOOTHPICKS

H • Rather than discard bottles that once contained hot pepper seasoning, wash with hot water, dry, and use them to store toothpicks. The openings are just the right size to permit the toothpicks to come out.

TOMATOES

G • If you're forced to take in a crop of pinkish or green garden fruits because of the sudden frost, wrap them in brown paper and store them in a cool, dark place.

H • Did you know that refrigerated tomatoes absorb odors more readily than other fruits? Store them wrapped in plastic or enameled containers, Baggies, or covered glass.

H • Did you know that equal parts of tomato juice and vinegar will remove that skunk smell from your dog?

H • In that hopelessly black frying pan, let some tomato juice soak for 30 to 45 minutes. The pan will then wash clean as new.

TURMERIC

M • Turmeric is most often met in pickles and in curries (which it colors with its brilliant yellow). The *U. S. Dispensatory* says that oil of turmeric yields curcumen, which dissolves cholestrin, a component of bile and gallstones; it therefore is protective to the gallbladder.

TURNIPS

Until recently turnips were syruped for use in coughs, bronchial • F
disorders, and hoarseness. Eaten raw and thoroughly chewed,
they're a wonderful tooth cleanser. Cut the roots in thin, long
strips and chew each slowly. A delicious taste. Include them in a
salad.

If you cook turnips, steam lightly, broil, or bake them. No odors • F
and no gas problems arise until you boil them in hot water. (Then
you're really in hot water.) Properly heated, they may be substituted for potato and eaten following a cold salad and before meat
or fish.

Turnips are a gold mine of blood-fortifying minerals, of calcium, • F
potassium, iron, sodium, and especially sulfur. A seventy-year-old
customer of mine told me that the secret of his still almost un-
grayed hair was that he ate a lot of uncooked turnips, radishes,
cabbage, and carrots.

A little known fact: turnip greens contain the highest amount of • F
calcium of all vegetables. One pound offers 1176 mg. compared to
lettuce (69 mg.), cabbage (152 mg.), and celery (143 mg.). Until
one is used to them, the leaves should be steamed for about 20 to
25 minutes, then for less and less cooking time. Or convert them
into a juice with dandelion leaves, carrots, and celery, and you
have a superb means of nourishing the body's bone structure,
especially that of children. These greens contain 3 times as much
vitamin C as orange or tomato juice.

UNKNOWN NUTRIENTS

When I meet a person who indulges in processed foods, and who • F
says, "A vitamin-and-mineral pill makes up for it," I set him
thinking with one idea: nutritional science has not yet identified,
much less isolated, all the nutrients needed by our bodies. We can
put into a pill only what we know. How many unknown nutrients

do we eat every week, perhaps in common foods like the apple we munched on yesterday or the cabbage we had for dinner? Why risk leaving unknown essentials out of our diet? Perhaps science will never identify all the nutrients.

UNSAFE COOKING UTENSILS

ALUMINUM:

H • There has been too much incriminating evidence against the use of aluminum cooking ware, documented for the past 20 years, to warrant continued use. Dietitians of certain hospitals are directed to refrain as much as possible from aluminum utensils. One doctor has stated that 1 of every 3 persons is sensitive to aluminum. In 1946, the Lee Foundation for Nutritional Research reported that aluminum salts from some baking powders, and aluminum acetate in perspiration deodorants, lessen the body's calcium and phosphorous.

Fruit juices will dissolve the aluminum from cooking utensils, creating severe abdominal disturbances. Doctors have reported such situations with patients who had eaten rhubarb which had been cooked in aluminum ware.

One man who complained of worsening abdominal pains, constipation, and headaches showed a marked improvement within 2 months after discarding his aluminum cooking utensils. In 1934, patients whose stomach, intestinal, kidney, or liver ills were attributed to their cooking foods in aluminum were reported completely cured after changing to glass or enamel cooking utensils.

Tests made at one Detroit hospital showed that aluminum is toxic and contaminates food. Jell-o made and cooled in an aluminum dish will taste unpleasantly bitter. Let lemonade stand overnight in an aluminum pan and it, too, will taste bitter. Cherries and grapes, boiled in an aluminum pot and left standing overnight, will make small holes in the pot. Cook cranberries a few minutes and they'll turn black, applesauce will turn dark green, and butterscotch filling will turn from dark brown to dark green. Mayonnaise dressing prepared in an aluminum utensil will assume a brown color. When cabbage and peeled potatoes are cooked in an aluminum pot, a harmful chemical change takes

place. The cabbage blackens the pot and the potatoes turn deep yellow to black.

An experiment: boil 2 quarts of water for ½ hour in an aluminum container. Repeat in either a porcelain or stainless steel utensil. Allow the water to cool and place goldfish in each container. Correct! Those in the aluminum utensil died within 4 hours; the others lived.

It has been reported that a greater loss of vitamin C occurs in foods that are cooked in aluminum than in those cooked in glass or enamel containers.

(Aluminum can be found sometimes in baking powders, city drinking water, pickles, commercially baked goods, in children's aspirin, in bases for false teeth preparations, and in drugs.)

LOW-FIRED CERAMICS:

Unglazed ceramics should not be used for cooking because, being porous, they absorb food which can then feed bacteria.
High-fired glazes on pottery and china are not dangerous. One

can usually tell high-fired pottery by tapping one's ring against it. A ringing sound indicates high firing; a plunky sound may indicate low firing.

Low-firing glazes are usually made from lead, which is very poisonous. The zinc glaze of some crockery and earthenware contains as much as 2 percent of the highly dangerous lead. Lead-based glazes are yellowish and are often used for bright, decorative, warm colors. Commercially made United States products contain no lead, but many handmade imports do. (By the way, I've been told that most pencils which are painted yellow are painted with lead-based paint! Do not let children chew on them!)

MICROWAVE OVENS:

Microwave ovens are not recommended; until proven *entirely* safe, they should be avoided. Certainly this type of oven is neither the time saver nor the performer of all cooking tasks one has been led by advertising to believe.

These "fast" ovens employ "cold" microwaves which, when absorbed by foods, are converted to heat. But the greatest danger is that human flesh and bones also absorb these dangerous waves.

True, it takes prolonged exposure to a high-intensity microwave radiation—1,000 milliwatts per square centimeter (1,000 mw/cm^2)—to yield a lethal dose. But the evidence has shown that 100 mw/cm^2 causes irreversible cataracts, and even 10 mw/cm^2 may produce testicular malfunction in laboratory animals. And effects on chromosomes have been reported as well.

Early in 1973, the federal government was sufficiently concerned to fund various research projects to ascertain the effects of microwaves upon the central nervous system, heart, and liver, and the degree of change in body proteins, enzymes, and genes. As yet, there is no unchallengeable *safe* level of microwave radiation emission.

At army bases signs are posted near microwave ovens to warn wearers of cardiac pacemaker implants of possible harm from radiation.

In some cities, a similar warning must also be posted near microwave ovens in restaurants. For these reasons alone, the manufacturers of ovens should be required to attach a permanent, large bold red tag on all such equipment. (Indeed, the pacemaker patient should actually leave the kitchen when a "fast" oven is in use.)

Further warnings that should but do not now appear on the label: the hazard of burns. Even though the door's sealing surface is undamaged, a radiation leak is always possible. Keep ovens out of the reach of children. Avoid peering into them while in use.

Why take a chance? Don't cook with microwave ovens.

TEFLON:

Teflon was much used in industry for wire insulating, chemical equipment, and electrical applications before it entered the kitchen. Unheated, it caused no problem, but once it became hot, it became extremely dangerous. Heated Teflon, when inhaled into the respiratory tract, caused serious illness, characterized by an influenzalike ailment with accompanying feverish chills and headache. This danger has been observed in factories where Teflon has been heated to over 500°. Similarly, when a Teflon-coated pot is long heated at a high temperature, or a hot iron remains on a Teflon-treated ironing board cover, there's a good chance someone will be adversely affected. Several years ago, a spacecraft company issued a warning: "Do not breathe the fumes arising from heating Teflon in any circumstances." A factory worker, according to a medical journal, was so violently poisoned by the fumes of his cigarette burning on a sheet of Teflon that he required immediate hospital attention to save his life.

There is, therefore, a danger of releasing the poisonous fumes when heating Teflon ware at high temperatures, or when the frying pan is accidentally overheated. It is also dangerous when it is scratched. In the absence of complete safety, one should seek other wares for the preparation of food.

ACCEPTABLE WARE

ENAMELWARE:

Buy a good- to best-grade of enamelware and keep it as long as it remains unchipped. Recent outbreaks of poisoning were due to the relatively large amounts of the more soluble antimony triox-

• H

ide in cheap enamels. Acid foods will disintegrate the enamel matrix which gives up small amounts of the poisonous metal to foods, and the use of such cheap enameled ware needs to be discontinued to prevent a heath hazard. Vinegar and other acid foods will cause the food to absorb the chemical, as noted by the power of lemonade's citric acid to attack the walls of the utensil.

STAINLESS STEEL:

Stainless steelware is quite acceptable. Some people recommend those pans with copper bottoms. The important thing is to buy good-quality merchandise. The stainless steel must contain a minimum of 11½ percent of chromium.

GLASS:

Glass is the best choice. Such ware may be a little more expensive but for health it is worth any price.

VANILLA

F • The use of vanilla for flavoring and medicine was taught to us by Mexican Indians. It is quieting to the stomach, helps expel wind, and aids the diuretic function.
Vanilla, by the way, is the dried fruit of an orchid.

VINEGAR

F • Inventory your herb-spice shelf. Remove the outdated and weak-flavored herbs and add these to an ever-waiting jar of cider vinegar.

M • Your basil, mint, and other herb vinegars (using the cider or brown variety as a base) relieve dryness and itching of the skin. For sunburn, pat on with cotton or a soft cloth. Equal parts of herb vinegar and spirits of turpentine make a good liniment for bruises.

An effective and inexpensive cleaning fluid for mirrors and windows: half-fill a clean spray bottle with water and add equal parts of household ammonia and white vinegar to fill. • **H**

A solution of salt and vinegar will remove fruit stains and unpleasant odors from the hands. • **H**

A small bowl of vinegar placed in an inconspicuous corner of the living room will absorb your guests' tobacco smoke. • **H**

Water bottles, thermos jugs, baby bottles, and decanters clean better if you shake a little vinegar in them first and then rinse. • **H**

Use a half-and-half solution of vinegar and water to remove grease and oil from the object you're going to paint. Apply with a cloth lightly dampened with the solution. • **H**

Hot vinegar will easily remove decals from windows and cupboards. • **H**

Hot vinegar removes freshly dried paint from windows. • **H**

VITAMINS

I believe that our everyday natural foods are the only proper source of vitamins, minerals, enzymes, and other growth and health-preserving factors. • **F**

It is quite easy to prepare your own food supplements. Your only cost is for 100 empty gelatin capsules , obtainable from your druggist, and a small amount of powdered leaf tops of various vegetables and ever-present herbs. . . . • **F**

WATERCRESS

Watercress's nutritive composition is similar to that of nasturtiums. One pound of fresh (raw) watercress has 7.7 grams protein, • **F**

885 mg. calcium, 21,450 units of vitamin A, and amounts of thiamin, riboflavin, and niacin greater than those in 5 eggs. It abounds in trace minerals of potassium, copper, and manganese, and especially in vitamin C (350 mg.), which helps to prevent not only scurvy but also hardening of the arteries by keeping the small blood vessels flexible.

WHEAT GERM

F • Wheat germ is a highly touted partial food which is but a meager speck of the entire wheat kernel. Though advertised as a tonic and a wonder food, it represents but a fraction of the entire food. (See CEREAL, LECITHIN, WHEAT GRAINS.)

WHEAT GRAINS

F • Sprouted wheat grains are rich sources of vitamins A, G, and especially the B-complex factors, choline and inositol, which help prevent fatty deposits in the arterial walls, and also E which helps to prevent sterility, miscarriage, arthritic tendencies, and unaccountable pains in muscles, soft tissues, and nerves. The sprouts abound in high-powered, essential amino acids and 11 blood-fortifying major minerals. (See SPROUTS.)

WINDOWS

G • Make use of the sills for your pots of plants. (See HERBS and PLANTS.)

H • If you do have a window garden, then protect the windowsills by coating them with wax. This protects the paint, and the water can be completely wiped off.

H • You do not need store-bought items to clean your windows. To each quart of water, add 1 tablespoonful of ammonia and/or 2 of vinegar. Rubbing alcohol is a very good window cleaner for especially cold days.

WITCH HAZEL

An excellent remedy for a sudden headache or sore eyes. Prepare a compress of the previously chilled liquid and place over the forehead or the closed eyes for a few minutes.

• **M**

For bee and insect bites, apply the cold solution.

• **M**

Sore muscles call for a rub with equal parts of rubbing alcohol and witch hazel.

• **M**

X

X-RATED FOODS

all strong spices
candy bars
celery salt
chili
cookies
curry
garlic salt
ice cream
mayonnaise
  (unless homemade)
monosodium glutamate
mustard
onions
pepper
processed food, including
  processed cheese
soft drinks
Tabasco sauce
Worcestershire sauce

• **F**

FIVE WHITE ENEMIES: salt
sugar
polished rice
white bread (bleached flour)
white vinegar

YOGURT

F • The past few years have seen yogurt skyrocketing in popularity. It is often eaten instead of sour cream and appears on the market in many flavors (which are needless and add to the food's cost). With cow's milk hardly suited to our digestive system, interesting that we digest yogurt 90 to 95 percent and milk only 44 percent. A complete and satisfying meal is a large vegetable salad, 2 tablespoonsful of yogurt, and 1 or 2 slices of homemade bread.

1. Yogurt should be made only from raw milk. Quick scalding destroys the one enzyme which causes souring but the other enzymes are undamaged. A starter is often used and powdered milk is usually added. Half a cup of powdered skim milk blended with a quart of milk yields a more rigid texture. The mixture may be poured into sterilized jelly glasses and the heat slowly brought to between 100° and 120°. In 4 to 6 hours the milk is custardlike.

2. Slowly bring 5½ cups of milk to 115° and add it to a previous blend of 4 tablespoonsful powdered skim milk and ½ glass yogurt. Warm again to 115°, fill the glasses, and cover with accompanying lid or a heavy towel, or place the glasses in a Styrofoam box with lid. When cool (in about 4 hours), cover the glasses with foil or wax paper and elastics. Refrigerate. When started with yogurt or yogurt culture, the milk is *not* scalded. (A starting culture may be purchased at health food stores.)

3. Beat into a pint of water 1½ cups powdered skim milk, 3 tablespoonsful yogurt, and one large can of evaporated milk. When smooth, add a quart of water and pour into glasses and put them into a pan previously set on the stove. Fill the pan with warm water which should come almost to the tops of the glasses. Heat to warm or simmer and maintain a heat between 105° and 125° for about 3 hours or until the yogurt thickens. Place individual covers over the glasses and keep in refrigerator until needed.

The disease-preventive properties of yogurt are too little known. • **M**
Not only is it of benefit in eliminating putrefaction in the intestines, but the lactic acid which yogurt produces encourages the development of beneficial intestinal bacteria while preventing the growth of the disease-producing ones. Nutritional scientists believe it has strong anticancer properties, because of the potent antitumor activity of the *Lactobacillus Bulgaricus* organism.
Not only is yogurt's protein far easier to digest than milk's, and its calcium content more adequately assimilated by the senior generation, but it produces far fewer gas disturbances because the harmful bacteria cannot live in the lactic acid. Thus yogurt's power to remove toxins from the system. And, too, the B-complex factors that yogurt generously creates in the intestinal tract keep that area clean and in good working order.

You can make your own mildly reasonable facsimile of yogurt • **F**
(actually a curdled milk or clabber) by placing some raw milk in a sterilized wide-mouth jar and covering with a paper towel or cheesecloth. Let stand in a warm area (average 80°) for 1½ to 2 days and stir occasionally to thoroughly mix the cream. When thickened, refrigerate.
This simple method requires no previous boiling of the raw milk which destroys practically all the beneficial bacteria.

ZUCCHINI

Never peel—peeling wastes nutrients. Add thin unpeeled slices to • **F**
a vegetable salad.
Steam or bake but never boil-spoil in a pot of hot water.

A FINAL NOTE TO MY READERS

If you have any money-saving or health-saving suggestions that I have not mentioned here, please send them to me c/o Barre Publishing so that I can include them in the next edition of *Kitchen Tricks*.

141

GARDENS AND GARDENING

HERBS AND SPICES, 121

HOUSEHOLD TIPS